First World War
and Army of Occupation
War Diary
France, Belgium and Germany

36 DIVISION
109 Infantry Brigade
Royal Inniskilling Fusiliers
11th Battalion
4 October 1915 - 21 February 1918

WO95/2510/5

The Naval & Military Press Ltd
www.nmarchive.com
Published in association with The National Archives

Published by

The Naval & Military Press Ltd

Unit 10 Ridgewood Industrial Park,

Uckfield, East Sussex,

TN22 5QE England

Tel: +44 (0) 1825 749494

www.naval-military-press.com

www.nmarchive.com

This diary has been reprinted in facsimile from the original. Any imperfections are inevitably reproduced and the quality may fall short of modern type and cartographic standards.

© Crown Copyright
Images reproduced by permission of The National Archives, London, England, 2015.

Contents

Document type	Place/Title	Date From	Date To
Heading	WO95/2510/5		
Heading	36th Division 109th Infy Bde 11th Bn Roy. Innis. Fus. Oct 1915-Feb 1918		
Heading	War Diary Of 11th. (Service) Batt. Royal Inniskilling Fusrs. From 4th October 1915 To 31st October 1915 (Volume No 1)		
War Diary	Bramshott	04/10/1915	05/10/1915
War Diary	Folkestone	06/10/1915	06/10/1915
War Diary	Boulogne	07/10/1915	07/10/1915
War Diary	Cardonnette	08/10/1915	21/10/1915
War Diary	Candas	22/10/1915	25/10/1915
War Diary	Pouchevillers	26/10/1915	26/10/1915
War Diary	Hedauville	27/10/1915	31/10/1915
Miscellaneous	11th. (S) Bn. Rl. Inniskilling Fusrs. Nominal Roll Of Officers Who Came Out With The Battalion Appendix I		
Map	Appendix 2		
Heading	War Diary Of 11th. (Service) Batt. Royal Inniskilling Fusrs. From 1st November 1915 To 30th November 1915 (Volume No. 2)		
War Diary	Hedauville	01/11/1915	03/11/1915
War Diary	Candas	04/11/1915	30/11/1915
Heading	War Diary Of 11th. (Service) Batt. Royal Inniskilling Fusrs. From 1st December 1915 To 31st December 1915 (Volume No. 3)		
War Diary	Brucamps	01/12/1915	31/12/1915
Heading	11th R. Innis K Fus Vol 4		
Heading	War Diary Of 11th. (Service) Battalion Royal Inniskilling Fusiliers. From. 1st January 1916 To 31st January 1916 (Volume 4)		
War Diary	Brucamps	01/01/1916	05/01/1916
War Diary	Canaples	06/01/1916	31/01/1916
Heading	War Diary Of 11th. (Ser) Bn. Royal Inniskilling Fusiliers. From 1st February, 1916 To 29th. February, 1916 (Volume 5)		
War Diary	Canaples	01/02/1916	07/02/1916
War Diary	Toutencourt	08/02/1916	08/02/1916
War Diary	Forceville	09/02/1916	12/02/1916
War Diary	Forceville And Trenches	13/02/1916	20/02/1916
War Diary	Mailly Maillet And Trenches	20/02/1916	24/02/1916
War Diary	Forceville	25/02/1916	27/02/1916
War Diary	Trenches	28/02/1916	29/02/1916
Map			
Map	Appendix 2		
Heading	War Diary Of 11th. (S.) Bn. Rl. Inniskilling Fusiliers From 1st March 1916 To 31st March 1916 (Volume No 6)		
War Diary	Trenches	01/03/1916	02/03/1916
War Diary	Forceville	03/03/1916	04/03/1916
War Diary	Mesnil	05/03/1916	06/03/1916
War Diary	Trenches	07/03/1916	10/03/1916

Type	Description	From	To
War Diary	Mesnil	11/03/1916	14/03/1916
War Diary	Trenches	15/03/1916	20/03/1916
War Diary	Mesnil	21/03/1916	26/03/1916
War Diary	Trenches	27/03/1916	31/03/1916
Miscellaneous	O.C. 11th R Inniskilling Fus	20/03/1916	20/03/1916
Operation(al) Order(s)	Operation Order No. 8 By Lieut. Colonel, W.F. Hessey, Commanding, 11th. (S) Bn. Rl. Inniskilling Fus. 21.3.16	21/03/1916	21/03/1916
Operation(al) Order(s)	Operation Order No. 9 By Lieut-Col W.F. Hessey Comdg. 11th (S) Bn. Rl. Inniskilling Fusiliers. 27.3.16	27/03/1916	27/03/1916
Heading	War Diary Of 11th. (Service) Battalion Royal Inniskilling Fusrs. From-1st April 1916 To-30th April 1916 (Volume No. 7)		
War Diary	Trenches	01/04/1916	02/04/1916
War Diary	Mesnil	03/04/1916	08/04/1916
War Diary	Trenches	09/04/1916	14/04/1916
War Diary	Mesnil	15/04/1916	20/04/1916
War Diary	Martinsart Wood Etc	21/04/1916	23/04/1916
War Diary	Martinsart Wood	24/04/1916	24/04/1916
War Diary	Trenches	25/04/1916	30/04/1916
Heading	War Diary Of 11th. (Service) Battalion Royal Inniskilling Fusiliers. From 1st May 1916 To 31st May 1916. (Volume No. 8)		
War Diary	Martinsart And Martinsart Wood	01/05/1916	07/05/1916
War Diary	Varennes	08/05/1916	31/05/1916
Heading	109th Brigade. 36th Division. 1/11th Battalion Royal Inniskilling Fusiliers June 1916		
War Diary	Varennes	01/06/1916	16/06/1916
War Diary	Aveluy Wood	17/06/1916	23/06/1916
War Diary	Forceville	24/06/1916	27/06/1916
War Diary	Martinsart	28/06/1916	28/06/1916
War Diary	Trenches Thiepval Wood	29/06/1916	30/06/1916
Miscellaneous	Appendix 1. War Diary, For Month June, 1916		
Heading	109th Brigade. 36th Division. 1/11th Battalion Royal Inniskilling Fusiliers July 1916		
War Diary	Thiepval Wood	01/07/1916	02/07/1916
War Diary	Martinsart Wood	02/07/1916	03/07/1916
War Diary	Hedauville	03/07/1916	05/07/1916
War Diary	Herissart	05/07/1916	09/07/1916
War Diary	Fienvillers	10/07/1916	10/07/1916
War Diary	Conteville	11/07/1916	11/07/1916
War Diary	Berguette	12/07/1916	12/07/1916
War Diary	Racquinghem	12/07/1916	13/07/1916
War Diary	Setques	13/07/1916	21/07/1916
War Diary	Bollezeele	21/07/1916	23/07/1916
War Diary	Bois De Ploegsteert	23/07/1916	31/07/1916
Map			
Miscellaneous	Report From The Officer Commanding, 11th (S) Bn. Rl. Inniskilling Fusiliers Re Operations 27th June-To July 1916	06/07/1916	06/07/1916
Miscellaneous	Special Order Of The Day By Lieut-General Sir, T.L.N. Morland" K.C.B., D.S.O., 3rd. July, 1916	03/07/1916	03/07/1916
Miscellaneous	Special Order Of The Day. By Major-General, O.S.W. Nugent, D.S.O. Commanding 36th. (Ulster) Division	03/07/1916	03/07/1916
Miscellaneous	109th (Ulster) Brigade. Order Of The Day By Brigadier General R.G. Shutter, D.S.O.	03/07/1916	03/07/1916

Miscellaneous	City Hall, Belfast, 20th July, 1916	31/07/1916	31/07/1916
Heading	War Diary Of 11th (S) Battalion Royal Inniskilling Fusiliers For Month Of August, 1916 Vol 9		
War Diary	Ploegsteert Wood	01/08/1916	03/08/1916
War Diary	Romarin	03/08/1916	09/08/1916
War Diary	Ploegsteert Wood	09/08/1916	15/08/1916
War Diary	Romarin	15/08/1916	21/08/1916
War Diary	Ploegsteert Wood	21/08/1916	28/08/1916
War Diary	Romarin	28/08/1916	31/08/1916
Heading	War Diary Of The 11th (Service) Battalion Royal Inniskilling Fusiliers From 1st September, 1916 To 30th September, 1916 (Volume XII)		
War Diary	Romarin	01/09/1916	03/09/1916
War Diary	Ploegsteert Wood	03/09/1916	06/09/1916
War Diary	Romarin	06/09/1916	07/09/1916
War Diary	Dranoutre	08/09/1916	30/09/1916
Miscellaneous	Report On Raid On Enemy Trenches Carried Out By 11th (S) Bn. Royal Inniskilling Fusiliers On Night 15th/16th September, 1916	16/09/1916	16/09/1916
Map	App no 1		
Heading	War Diary Of 11th (Service) Battalion Royal Inniskilling Fusiliers From 1st October, 1916 To 31st October, 1916 (Volume XIII)		
War Diary	Aircraft Farm N.32 Central	01/10/1916	06/10/1916
War Diary	Spanbroek Sector	06/10/1916	12/10/1916
War Diary	Wakefield Huts Dranoutre	13/10/1916	18/10/1916
War Diary	Spanbroek Sector	18/10/1916	24/10/1916
War Diary	Derry Camp N32 Central	24/10/1916	29/10/1916
War Diary	Spanbroek Sector	30/10/1916	31/10/1916
Heading	War Diary Of 11th Royal Inniskilling Fusiliers, From 1st November 1916 To 30th November 1916. Vol 14		
War Diary	Spanbroek Sector	01/11/1916	05/11/1916
War Diary	Dranoutre	05/11/1916	10/11/1916
War Diary	Spanbroek Sector	11/11/1916	16/11/1916
War Diary	Derry Camp N32 Central	17/11/1916	17/11/1916
War Diary	Derry Camp	18/11/1916	23/11/1916
War Diary	Spanbroek Sector	23/11/1916	29/11/1916
War Diary	Dranoutre	29/11/1916	30/11/1916
Miscellaneous	Scheme To Raid Enemy Trenches Left Sub-Sector, 109th Brigade Appendix no.1	05/11/1916	05/11/1916
Miscellaneous	11th (S) Bn. Rl. Inniskilling Fusiliers. Appendix No 2		
Miscellaneous	Report On Raid On Enemy's Trenches Carried Out By 11th (S) Battalion Royal Inniskilling Fus. On Night 16/17th November, 1916 Appendix No 3	17/11/1916	17/11/1916
Miscellaneous	Battalion Routine Orders By Lieut-Col. A.G. Pratt Commanding 11th (S) Bn. Rl. Innis. Fuslrs. Appendix no. 4	18/11/1916	18/11/1916
War Diary	War Diary Of 11th Battalion Royal Inniskilling Fusiliers From 1st December 1916 To 31st December 1916 Vol 15		
Heading	War Diary Of The 11th (Service) Battalion Royal Inniskilling Fusiliers. From 1st December, 1916 To 31st December, 1916 (Volume XV)		
War Diary	Wakefield Huts Dranoutre	01/12/1916	04/12/1916
War Diary	Kortepyp	04/12/1916	05/12/1916
War Diary	Douve Sector Bois De Pleogsteert	05/12/1916	13/12/1916

War Diary	Hyde Park Corner Bois De Pleogsteert	13/12/1916	21/12/1916
War Diary	Douve Sector Bois De Pleogsteert	21/12/1916	28/12/1916
War Diary	Hyde Park Corner Bois De Pleogsteert	29/12/1916	31/12/1916
Heading	War Diary Of The 11th (Service) Battalion Royal Inniskilling Fusiliers. From 1st January, 1917 To 31st January, 1917 (Volume XVI)		
War Diary	Galleries Hyde Park Corner	01/01/1917	06/01/1917
War Diary	Douve Sector	06/01/1917	14/01/1917
War Diary	Galleries Hyde Park Corner	14/01/1917	22/01/1917
War Diary	Douve Sector	22/01/1917	30/01/1917
War Diary	Galleries Hyde Park Corner	30/01/1917	31/01/1917
Heading	War Diary Of 11th Battalion Royal Innis. Fusiliers. From 1st February 1917 To 28th February 1917. Vol 17		
Heading	War Diary Of The 11th. (Service) Battalion Royal Inniskilling Fusiliers. From 1st. February, 1917. To 31st. February, 1917 (Volume XVII)		
War Diary	Galleries Hyde Park Corner	01/02/1917	07/02/1917
War Diary	Douve Sector	07/02/1917	15/02/1917
War Diary	Galleries Hyde Park Corner	15/02/1917	23/02/1917
War Diary	Douve Sector	23/02/1917	25/02/1917
War Diary	Galleries Hyde Park Corner	25/02/1917	26/02/1917
War Diary	Phincboom	27/02/1917	28/02/1917
Heading	War Diary Of 11th Battalion Royal Innis. Fusiliers, From 1st March 1917. To 31st March 1917. Vol 18		
War Diary	Phincboom	01/03/1917	20/03/1917
War Diary	Blaringhem	21/03/1917	21/03/1917
War Diary	Martin-Au-Laert	22/03/1917	22/03/1917
War Diary	St. Martin-Au-Laert	22/03/1917	22/03/1917
War Diary	Westrecourt Val-D'Acquin	23/03/1917	23/03/1917
War Diary	Bouvelinghem	24/03/1917	29/03/1917
War Diary	Westbecourt Val-De-Acquin	30/03/1917	30/03/1917
War Diary	Bouvelinghem	31/03/1917	31/03/1917
Heading	War Diary Of 11th Battalion Royal Inniskilling Fusiliers, From 1st April 1917 Till 30th April 1917. Vol 19		
War Diary	Westbecourt	01/04/1917	04/04/1917
War Diary	St. Martin-Au-Laert	05/04/1917	05/04/1917
War Diary	Hazebrouck	06/04/1917	06/04/1917
War Diary	Kemmel Hill	07/04/1917	07/04/1917
War Diary	Span Broek Left Sub-Sector	08/04/1917	14/04/1917
War Diary	Kemmel	15/04/1917	19/04/1917
War Diary	Spanbroek Right Sub-Sector	20/04/1917	25/04/1917
War Diary	Kemmel	26/04/1917	30/04/1917
Heading	War Diary Of 11th. Battalion Royal Inniskilling Fusiliers, From 1st. May, 1917. Till 31st. May, 1917 Vol 20		
War Diary	Spanbroek Left Sub-Sector	01/05/1917	08/05/1917
War Diary	Kemmel	09/05/1917	13/05/1917
War Diary	Wakefield Huts Dranoutre	14/05/1917	31/05/1917
Heading	War Diary For Month Of June 1917. 11th. Royal Inniskilling Fusiliers. Vol 21		
Heading	War Diary Of The 11th (Service) Battalion Royal Inniskilling Fusiliers. From 1st. June, 1917 To 30th June, 1917. (Volume XXI)		
War Diary	Dranoutre	01/06/1917	01/06/1917
War Diary	Mont Noir	02/06/1917	06/06/1917

War Diary	Wakefield Huts Spanbroek Sector	07/06/1917	07/06/1917
War Diary	Blue Line	07/06/1917	07/06/1917
War Diary	Spanbroek Sector	08/06/1917	08/06/1917
War Diary	Wakefield Huts	09/06/1917	12/06/1917
War Diary	Mont Noir	13/06/1917	17/06/1917
War Diary	Buterfly Farm	18/06/1917	18/06/1917
War Diary	Oosttaverne Sub Sector	19/06/1917	24/06/1917
War Diary	Support Trenches	25/06/1917	27/06/1917
War Diary	Garden Farm	28/06/1917	30/06/1917
Miscellaneous	11th (S) Battn. Royal Inniskilling Fusiliers Special Order Of The Day	06/06/1917	06/06/1917
Miscellaneous	11th (S) Battn. Royal Inniskilling Fusiliers Casualties	07/06/1917	07/06/1917
Miscellaneous	Narrative Of Operations In Attack On Enemy Position On 7th June 1917	14/06/1917	14/06/1917
Miscellaneous	11th (S) Battn. Royal Inniskilling Fusiliers. Special Order Of The Day	08/06/1917	08/06/1917
Miscellaneous		13/06/1917	13/06/1917
Miscellaneous	11th (S) Battn. Royal Inniskilling Fusiliers. Recommendations For Immediate Reward In Order Of Merit	14/06/1917	14/06/1917
Miscellaneous			
Operation(al) Order(s)	Operation Orders No. 1 By Lieut-Col A.C. Pratt. D.S.O. Commanding 11th (S) Bn. Rl. Inniskilling Fusiliers.		
Heading	11th Royal Inniskilling Fusiliers. War Diary For Month Of July, 1917. Vol 22		
War Diary	Rouge Croix Strazeele	01/07/1917	05/07/1917
War Diary	Hondeghem	06/07/1917	06/07/1917
War Diary	Arques	07/07/1917	07/07/1917
War Diary	Alquines	08/07/1917	26/07/1917
War Diary	Winnezeele	27/07/1917	30/07/1917
War Diary	Watou Area	31/07/1917	31/07/1917
Heading	War Diary Of The 11th (S) Battalion Royal Inniskilling Fusiliers. From 1st August, 1917 To 31st. August, 1917 (Volume XXIII)		
Heading	War Diary 11th Royal Inniskilling Fusiliers. For Month Of August 1917. Vol 23		
Miscellaneous	To, Headquarters, 109th Inf. Brigade	01/09/1917	01/09/1917
War Diary	Watou	01/08/1917	03/08/1917
War Diary	Wieltje	04/08/1917	05/08/1917
War Diary	Vlamertinghe	06/08/1917	17/08/1917
War Diary	Winnizelle	18/08/1917	23/08/1917
War Diary	Barastre	25/08/1917	28/08/1917
War Diary	Neuville	29/08/1917	31/08/1917
Miscellaneous	Battalion Orders By Lieut-Col. A.C. Pratt D.S.O. Commanding 11th (S) Battn. Royal Inniskilling Fusiliers	03/08/1917	03/08/1917
Map	G.3.		
Miscellaneous	Message Form		
Map	J.3		
Miscellaneous	Message Form		
Miscellaneous	Instructions For The Offensive By Lieut-Col. A.C. Pratt D.S.O. Commanding 11th (S) Battn. Royal Inniskilling Fusiliers	13/08/1917	13/08/1917
Miscellaneous	Battalion Orders By Major J.E.Knott. D.S.O. Commanding 11th (S) Battn. Royal Inniskilling Fusiliers	28/08/1917	28/08/1917

Heading	War Diary Of 11th Battalion Royal Inniskilling Fusiliers Period 1st September 1917 To 30th September 1917 Vol 24		
War Diary	Hermies Left Sub Sector	01/09/1917	05/09/1917
War Diary	Bertincourt	06/09/1917	12/09/1917
War Diary	Hermies Left Sub Sector	13/09/1917	20/09/1917
War Diary	Bertincourt	21/09/1917	28/09/1917
War Diary	Hermies Left Sub-Sector	29/09/1917	30/09/1917
Heading	To, 109th Inf. Bde	31/10/1917	31/10/1917
Heading	War Diary Of The 11th (Service) Battalion Royal Inniskilling Fusiliers. From 1st October, 1917. To 31st October, 1917 (Volume XXV)		
War Diary	Demicourt	01/10/1917	07/10/1917
War Diary	Bertincourt	08/10/1917	15/10/1917
War Diary	Demicourt	16/10/1917	23/10/1917
War Diary	Bertincourt	24/10/1917	31/10/1917
Heading	11th Inniskilling Fusiliers. War Diary For Period From 1st To 30th November, 1917 Vol 26		
Heading	War Diary Of The 11th (S) Battalion Royal Inniskilling Fusiliers 1st November 1917 To 30 November 1917 Volume XXVI		
War Diary	Hermies	01/11/1917	06/11/1917
War Diary	Bertincourt	07/11/1917	12/11/1917
War Diary	Hermies	13/11/1917	16/11/1917
War Diary	Velu Wood	17/11/1917	20/11/1917
War Diary	Enemy's Trenches	20/11/1917	22/11/1917
War Diary	Hermies	23/11/1917	24/11/1917
War Diary	Enemy's Trenches	25/11/1917	28/11/1917
War Diary	Bertincourt	28/11/1917	28/11/1917
War Diary	Beaulencourt	29/11/1917	29/11/1917
War Diary	Couy	30/11/1917	30/11/1917
Heading	11th Royal Inniskilling Fusiliers. War Diary For Month Of December 1917 Vol 27		
War Diary	Achiet-Le-Petit	01/12/1917	01/12/1917
War Diary	Barcourt	02/12/1917	02/12/1917
War Diary	Bertincourt	03/12/1917	04/12/1917
War Diary	Trenches	05/12/1917	09/12/1917
War Diary	Metz	10/12/1917	13/12/1917
War Diary	Sorel-Le-Grand	14/12/1917	15/12/1917
War Diary	Rocquigny	16/12/1917	16/12/1917
War Diary	Lucheux	17/12/1917	29/12/1917
War Diary	Moreuil	30/12/1917	31/12/1917
Heading	11th Royal Inniskilling Fusiliers. War Diary For Month Of January, 1918. Vol 28		
War Diary	Moreuil	01/01/1918	07/01/1918
War Diary	Villers Aux Erables	08/01/1918	09/01/1918
War Diary	Selente	10/01/1918	11/01/1918
War Diary	St Simon	12/01/1918	20/01/1918
War Diary	Trenches	21/01/1918	29/01/1918
War Diary	Artemps	30/01/1918	31/01/1918
Miscellaneous	Relief Orders By Major R.S. Knox, D.S.O. Commanding 10th (Service) Battalion Royal Inniskilling Fusiliers	17/01/1918	17/01/1918
Heading	11th Royal Inniskilling Fusiliers. War Diary For Month Of February, 1918. Vol 29		

Heading	War Diary Of 11th (S) Battn. Royal Inniskilling Fusiliers 20th February, 1918. Volume 29		
War Diary	Artemps	01/02/1918	07/02/1918
War Diary	Villeselve	08/02/1918	19/02/1918
War Diary	Cugny	20/02/1918	21/02/1918

worst 25/10/5 (s)

worst 25/10/5 (s)

36TH DIVISION
109TH INFY BDE

11TH BN ROY. INNIS. FUS.
OCT 1915- FEB 1918

DISBANDED

CONFIDENTIAL.

WAR DIARY

of

11th. (Service) Batt. ROYAL INNISKILLING FUSRS.

FROM 4th October, 1915   TO 31st October, 1915

(VOLUME No. 1.)

Army Form C. 2118.

WAR DIARY
INTELLIGENCE SUMMARY.
(Erase heading not required.)

Instructions regarding War Diaries and Intelligence Summaries are contained in F. S. Regs., Part II. and the Staff Manual respectively. Title pages will be prepared in manuscript.

Place	Date	Hour	Summary of Events and Information	Remarks and references to Appendices
BRAMSHOTT	4.10.15	—	Advance party left BRAMSHOTT Camp, LIPHOOK, SURREY, at 9am. Strength of Party 5 Officers and 109 other ranks. This included Transport and Machine Gun Section. The Party journeyed via SOUTHAMPTON — HAVRE to CARDONNETTE.	Strength of the Battalion landed in France 30 Officers 998 Oth. Ranks
BRAMSHOTT	5.10.15	—	"A" and "B" Companies left BRAMSHOTT CAMP at 5 p.m. — "C" & "D" Companies followed 40 minutes later. The Battalion, less Advance Party, 27 Officers and 889 other Ranks, entrained at LIPHOOK in 2 trains and left at 7 and 7.30 p.m. Arrived at FOLKESTONE and embarked on the Transport "St. SEIRIEL" at 12 midnight.	Attached "Appendice I" "Names of Officers who came out with
FOLKESTONE	6.10.15	—	The steamer left FOLKESTONE at 12.30 a.m. and crossed to BOULOGNE. Disembarked at BOULOGNE at 3am, and marched to OSTROHOVE Rest Camp, arriving there at 4.30 am where they remained for the day.	
BOULOGNE	7.10.15	—	The Battalion left BOULOGNE by train at 12 noon, arriving at FLESSELLES at 6 p.m. - detrained, the Battalion and marched to the village of CARDONNETTE arriving at 8.45 p.m. Here they were billeted and joined the Advance Party, who had arrived the day before.	
CARDONNETTE	8.10.15	—	Routine Work.	
"	9.10.15	—	Inspected by General Sir C.C.MONRO, K.C.B., Commanding 3rd Army, who complimented the Battalion on their smart appearance and fine physique.	

Army Form C. 2118.

WAR DIARY

INTELLIGENCE SUMMARY.

(Erase heading not required.)

Place	Date	Hour	Summary of Events and Information	Remarks and references to Appendices
CARDONNETTE	10.10.15	—	Routine Work	
"	11.10.15	—	Routine Work	
"	12.10.15	—	Routine Work	
"	13.10.15	—	Routine Work	
"	14.10.15	—	Routine Work	
"	15.10.15	—	Routine Work	
"	16.10.15	—	Routine Work	
"	17.10.15	—	Lecture by CHEMICAL ADVISER, 3rd Army, on Gas Helmets. The Battalion wore their gas helmets and had them tested with gas.	
"	18.10.15	—	Routine Work	
"	19.10.15	—	Routine Work	
"	20.10.15	—	Routine Work. Orders received at 6.30 p.m. to vacate CARDONNETTE and to be on the South side of DOULLENS - AMIENS Road by 12 noon the following day.	
"	21.10.15		The Battalion marched out of CARDONNETTE at 8 a.m. to a point EAST of FLESSELLES where it assembled with the other Battalions of the Brigade facing NORTH. The Brigade was ordered to march NORTH, across country in Artillery formation to a point NORTH.	

Continued on Page 3.

Army Form C. 2118.

3

WAR DIARY
INTELLIGENCE SUMMARY.
(Erase heading not required.)

Instructions regarding War Diaries and Intelligence Summaries are contained in F. S. Regs., Part II. and the Staff Manual respectively. Title pages will be prepared in manuscript.

Place	Date	Hour	Summary of Events and Information	Remarks and references to Appendices
CARDONNETTE	21.10.15	C.of	of NAMOUR. Afterwards the Battalion proceeded to CANDAS, arriving at 8.45 p.m. where it was billeted.	
CANDAS	22.10.15	-	Routine Work	
"	23.10.15	-	Routine Work	
"	24.10.15	-	Routine Work	
"	25.10.15	-	The Battalion left CANDAS at 8 a.m. for a week's instruction in the trenches. Arrived at POUCHEVILLERS at 12.30 p.m. and was billeted for the night.	
POUCHEVILLERS	26.10.15	-	Left POUCHEVILLERS at 8 a.m. marched to HEDAUVILLE arriving at 12 noon. Here the Battalion went under orders. While under instruction the Battalion was attached to 11th Infantry Brigade, 4th Division.	
HEDAUVILLE	27.10.15	-	"A" and "B" Company went into the trenches for 3 days. "A" Company was attached to the 1st Bn Rifle Brigade. "B" Company was attached to the 1st HAMPSHIRE REGT. The part of the line of trenches held was situated due NORTH of HAMEL. Sketch attached.	Appendice II. "Sketch F"
	28.10.15	-	"C" & "D" Companies, instruction in Camp.	
	29.10.15	-	- do -	Trenches occupied
	30.10.15	-	One Casualty in "A" Co-y. Lt Munson At Montgomery slight bullet wound in knee. "A" and "B" Companies returned from trenches to Camp. "C" & "D" Companies attached to 1st by Battalion when under instruction.	
			1st Bn. EAST LANCASHIRE REGT. "D" Company attached to a Battalion SOMERSETSHIRE LIGHT INFANTRY.	

Army Form C. 2118.

WAR DIARY
INTELLIGENCE SUMMARY.
(Erase heading not required.)

Instructions regarding War Diaries and Intelligence Summaries are contained in F. S. Regs., Part II. and the Staff Manual respectively. Title pages will be prepared in manuscript.

Place	Date	Hour	Summary of Events and Information	Remarks and references to Appendices
HEDAUVILLE	31.10.15	—	"C" and "D" Companies in trenches. "A" "D" Companies in Camp.	
			Strength of Battalion on 31.10.1915 — 30 Officers and 994 other Ranks.	
			Reference Maps:	
			HAVRE — FRANCE. 1/80000. SHEET. 19.	
			BOULOGNE } — " — 1/80000 — " — 3	
			OSTROHOVE }	
			All other FRENCH TOWNS — FRANCE. 1/80000, SHEET. 12.	

Larkin Major
COMDG. 11th (S.) Bn. RL. INNISKILLING FUS

11th.(S)Bn.Rl.Inniskilling Fuses.

Appendix I

NOMINAL ROLL OF OFFICERS WHO CAME OUT WITH THE BATTALION.

Rank	Surname	Christian name in Full	Date of Embarkation	Remarks
Lieut.Col.	Hessey,	William Francis	5.10.15.	
Major,	Leitrim,	The Earl of	4.10.15.	
"	Falls,	Charles Fausset	5.10.15.	
Captain,	Sewell,	William Tait,	"	
"	Myles,	James Sproule	"	
" & Adjt.	Moore,	William	"	
Captain	Butler,	Henry Cavendish	"	
"	Boyton,	James Godfrey	"	
"	Ballintine,	Jospeh	"	
"	Forde	Gordon Miller	"	
Lieut.	Wagentreiber,	William Harnett	"	
"	Gordon,	Herbert Crawford	"	
"	McCorkell	Barry Francis	"	
"	Orr	Robert Gerald	"	
"	Webb	George Henry	"	
"	Gallaugher	Henry	4.10.15.	
"	Falls	Cyril Bentham	5.10.15.	
"	Irvine	Gerard Mervyn Frederick	4.10.15.	
2nd.Lieut.	Craig	John Arnott Taylor	5.10.15.	
"	M'Ildowie	John Durie	"	
"	Hart	Andrew Chichester	"	
"	Williamson	William Robert	"	
"	Munn	Lionel Oulton Moore	"	
"	Knight,	William Madden	"	
"	Grant	Robert	"	
"	Rutledge	Laurence Hugh Nesbit	"	
"	Browne	Andrew Douglas Comyn	"	
"	Hanna	John Riddell Musgrove	"	
Lieut. R.A.M.C.	Crosbie	Douglas Edward	"	Medical Officer
Lieut & Quartermaster	Firth,	James Webster	"	

Leitrim Major
COMDG. 11th (S.) Bn. RL INNISKILLING FUS.

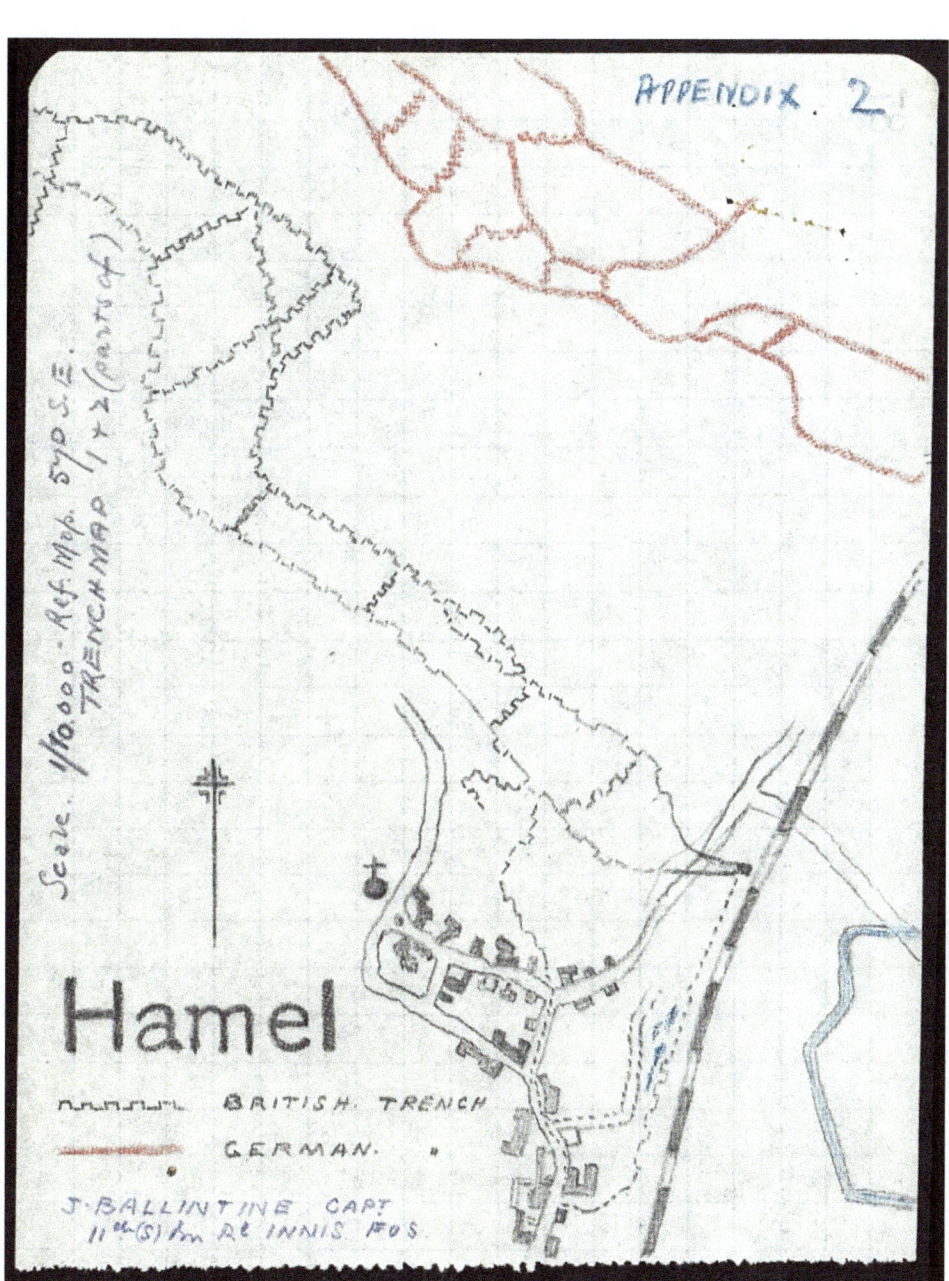

CONFIDENTIAL.

WAR DIARY

of

11th. (Service) Batt. ROYAL INNISKILLING FUSRS.

FROM *1st November 1915.* TO *30th November 1915*

(VOLUME No. *2*.)

Army Form C. 2118.

WAR DIARY

INTELLIGENCE SUMMARY.

(Erase heading not required.)

Instructions regarding War Diaries and Intelligence Summaries are contained in F. S. Regs., Part II. and the Staff Manual respectively. Title pages will be prepared in manuscript.

Place	Date	Hour	Summary of Events and Information	Remarks and references to Appendices
HEDAUVILLE	1.11.15	—	"C" and "D" Companies in trenches. "A" & "B" Companies in Camp.	
	2.11.15	—	"C" and "D" Companies came back to Camp from trenches at 4 p.m. Heavy rain all day.	
	3.11.15	—	The Battalion left HEDAUVILLE at 9 a.m. and marched via VARRENNES – LEALVILLERS – RANCHEVAL – BEAUQUESNE – BEAUVAL to CANDAS. Arriving at 4.45 p.m. and occupied billets. The men's boots were in a very bad condition, and the great coats wet though. Five men fell out on the march, two from sprained ankles caused by bad boots. A fine day.	
CANDAS	4.11.15	—	Routine Work.	
	5.11.15	—	Routine Work.	
	6.11.15	—	Routine Work. – 5 Officers & 50 Other Ranks to Brigade Headqrs for instruction in Bombing.	
	7.11.15	—	Routine Work.	
	8.11.15	—	Routine Work.	
	9.11.15	—	Routine Work.	
	10.11.15	—	Routine Work.	
	11.11.15	—	Routine Work.	
	12.11.15	—	Routine Work.	
	13.11.15	—	Routine Work.	

WAR DIARY

INTELLIGENCE SUMMARY.

(Erase heading not required.)

Army Form C. 2118.

Instructions regarding War Diaries and Intelligence Summaries are contained in F. S. Regs., Part II. and the Staff Manual respectively. Title pages will be prepared in manuscript.

Place	Date	Hour	Summary of Events and Information	Remarks and references to Appendices
CANDAS	14.11.15	—	Routine Work.	
	15.11.15	—	Routine Work. Snow fell.	
	16.11.15	—	Routine Work.	
	17.11.15	—	Routine Work.	
	18.11.15	—	Routine Work. Keen frost. Weather Cold.	
	19.11.15	—	Routine Work. " — " — " — "	
	20.11.15	—	Routine Work. ½ of the Battalion inoculated.	
	21.11.15	—	Routine Work. Remainder of Battalion inoculated. Still freezing & very cold.	
	22.11.15	—	Routine Work.	
	23.11.15	—	Routine Work.	
	24.11.15	—	Routine Work.	
	25.11.15	—	Routine Work.	
	26.11.15	—	Routine Work.	
	27.11.15	—	The Battalion left CANDAS at 8.30 am and marched via FIENVILLER – DOMART-en-PONTHIEU to BRUCAMPS. Arriving at 2.30 p.m. and occupied billets. Hard frost. cold.	
	28.11.15	—	Routine Work. 2nd Lieut. S.D. MILLER, on promotion for ROYAL HORSE GUARDS was taken on strength of the Battalion.	
	29.11.15	—	Routine Work. Heavy Rainfall.	
	30.11.15	—	Routine Work. Strength on this date. 31 Officers, 965 Other Ranks.	

REFERENCE MAP :- France 1/80,000. Sheet 12. AMIENS.

J. Brown Major
Comdg. 11th (S.) Bn. Rl. INNISKILLING Fus

CONFIDENTIAL.

WAR DIARY

of

11th. (Service) Batt. ROYAL INNISKILLING FUSRS.

FROM 1st December 1915   TO 31st December 1915.

(VOLUME No. 3.)

Army Form C. 2118.

WAR DIARY

INTELLIGENCE SUMMARY.

(Erase heading not required.)

Instructions regarding War Diaries and Intelligence Summaries are contained in F. S. Regs., Part II. and the Staff Manual respectively. Title pages will be prepared in manuscript.

Place	Date	Hour	Summary of Events and Information	Remarks and references to Appendices
BRUCAMPS	1.12.15	-	Routine Work	
"	2.12.15	-	Routine Work	
"	3.12.15	-	Routine Work	
"	4.12.15	-	Routine Work	
"	5.12.15	-	Routine Work	
"	6.12.15	-	Routine Work	
"	7.12.15	-	Routine Work	
"	8.12.15	-	Routine Work. Billets inspected by Divisional Commander, who was pleased with the cleanliness and sanitary arrangements of the village	
"	9.12.15	-	Routine Work	
"	10.12.15	-	Routine Work	
"	11.12.15	-	Routine Work	
"	12.12.15	-	Routine Work	
"	13.12.15	-	Routine Work	
"	14.12.15	-	Routine Work	
"	15.12.15	-	Goggles for each man of the Battalion received. Instructions in case of rapid mobilization received	

Army Form C. 2118.

WAR DIARY
INTELLIGENCE SUMMARY.
(Erase heading not required.)

Instructions regarding War Diaries and Intelligence Summaries are contained in F.S. Regs., Part II. and the Staff Manual respectively. Title pages will be prepared in manuscript.

Place	Date	Hour	Summary of Events and Information	Remarks and references to Appendices
BRUCAMPS	16.12.15	-	Routine Work.	
	17.12.15	-	Reinforcement from the Base received - 50 Other Ranks.	
	18.12.15	-	Routine Work.	
	19.12.15	-	Routine Work.	
	20.12.15	-	Routine Work.	
	21.12.15	-	Routine Work. LIEUT. COL. W.F. HESSEY took over Command of the Brigade during leave of absence of BRIGADIER GENERAL T.E. HICKMAN. MAJOR THE EARL OF LEITRIM took over the Command of the Battalion from LIEUT COL. W.F. HESSEY.	
	22.12.15	-	Routine Work.	
	23.12.15	-	Routine Work.	
	24.12.15	-	Routine Work.	
	25.12.15	-	Xmas Day. Holiday.	
	26.12.15	-	Sunday.	
	27.12.15	-	Boxing Day. Holiday.	
	28.12.15	-	Routine Work.	
	29.12.15	-	Routine Work.	

Army Form C. 2118.

WAR DIARY
INTELLIGENCE SUMMARY.

(Erase heading not required.)

Place	Date	Hour	Summary of Events and Information	Remarks and references to Appendices
BRUCAMPS	30.12.15	-	Routine Work	
	31.12.15	-	Routine Work	
			Strength of Battalion 31.12.1915 = 31 Officers. 989 other Ranks	
			REFERENCE MAP :- FRANCE. 1/80.000 SHEET. 12	

Jervis Major.
COMDG. 11th (S.) Bn. RL. INNISKILLING FUS.

11th R. Irenth? Fas?
Vol 4

Tan

Bl

S₂

CONFIDENTIAL.

WAR DIARY

of

11th. (SERVICE) BATTALION ROYAL INNISKILLING FUSILIERS.

FROM.   1st. January, 1916.   TO   31st. January, 1916.

(VOLUME 4.)

Army Form C. 2118.

WAR DIARY

INTELLIGENCE SUMMARY

(Erase heading not required.)

Place	Date	Hour	Summary of Events and Information	Remarks and references to Appendices
BRUCAMPS	1.1.16		Orders received for 2 Companies to proceed to CANAPLES and report to Officer Commanding, Royal Engineers at NAOURS.	
"	2.1.16		"B" and "D" Companies proceeded to CANAPLES at 10 am, and on arrival found that they could not be accomodated and had to billet at HALLOY.	
"	3.1.16		"B" and "D" Companies, Routine Work. Working Party for R.E.'s at CANAPLES	
"	4.1.16		"A" and "C" Companies, Routine Work	
"	5.1.16		same as for 3.1.16	
"			same as for 4.1.16	
CANAPLES	6.1.16		"A" and "C" Companies and Headquarters, proceeded to CANAPLES and joined "B" and "D" Companies who had already arrived there. The Battalion took over the Billets of the 18th MANCHESTER REGIMENT	
"	7.1.16		Routine Work, 1 Company Working Party for R.E.'s	
"	8.1.16		same as for 7.1.16	
"	9.1.16		Sunday	
"	10.1.16		Routine Work, 1 Company, Working Party for R.E."	
"	11.1.16		same as for 10.1.16	

WAR DIARY or INTELLIGENCE SUMMARY

Army Form C. 2118.

(Erase heading not required.)

Place	Date	Hour	Summary of Events and Information	Remarks and references to Appendices
CANAPLES	12.1.16		Routine Work. 1 Company Working Party for R.E's. Commander-in-Chief passed through the Village at 2.55 p.m.	
"	13.1.16		Routine work. 1 Company Working Party for R.E. "B" Company: 4 Officers and 181 Other Ranks proceeded to LONGUEVILLETTE to be stationed there for wood cutting.	
"	14.1.16		Routine Work. 1 Company Working Party for R.E's	
"	15.1.16		Same as for 14.1.16	
"	16.1.16		Sunday	
"	17.1.16		"A" Company at PERNOIS – "C" Company CANAPLES – "D" Company HALLOY, Working Parties (External)	
"	18.1.16		Same as for 17.1.16	
"	19.1.16		Same as for 18.1.16	
"	20.1.16		Same as for 19.1.16	
"	21.1.16		Same as for 20.1.16	
"	22.1.16		Same as for 21.1.16	
"	23.1.16		Sunday. 2 Officers and 33 Other Ranks transferred to 109th Bde Machine Gun Company.	
"	24.1.16		Same as for 22.1.16	

Army Form C. 2118.

WAR DIARY

~~INTELLIGENCE SUMMARY.~~

(Erase heading not required.)

Instructions regarding War Diaries and Intelligence Summaries are contained in F. S. Regs., Part II. and the Staff Manual respectively. Title pages will be prepared in manuscript.

Place	Date	Hour	Summary of Events and Information	Remarks and references to Appendices
CHIAPLES	25.1.16		Same as for 24.1.16	
"	26.1.16		Training in morning. Working in afternoon. Leave commences for Division at the rate of 1 per day for Battalion.	
"	27.1.16		Same as for 26.1.1916	
"	28.1.16		Same as for 27.1.1916	
"	29.1.16		Same as for 28.1.1916	
"	30.1.16		Commence training. Working Scheme Working parties discontinued	
"	31.1.16		Routine Work	

Strength of Battalion 31.1.16 Officers Other Ranks
30 — 959
+ Includes 2 Officers temporarily transferred to 136 Machine Gun Company

In the Field
31st January 1916

Lewin
Major
Comdg 11(S)Bn R Sussex Regt

1577 Wt.W10791/1773 500,000 1/15 D.D.&L. A.D.S.S./Forms/C. 2118.

CONFIDENTIAL.

WAR DIARY

of

11th.(Ser) BN. ROYAL INNISKILLING FUSILIERS.

From 1st. February, 1916   To 29th. February, 1916.

(Volume 5.)

Army Form C. 2118.

WAR DIARY
or
INTELLIGENCE SUMMARY.
(Erase heading not required.)

Instructions regarding War Diaries and Intelligence Summaries are contained in F. S. Regs., Part II. and the Staff Manual respectively. Title pages will be prepared in manuscript.

Place	Date	Hour	Summary of Events and Information	Remarks and references to Appendices
CANAPLES	1.2.16	—	B. Company rejoined from LONGUEVILLETTE. Routine Work. JL	
"	2.2.16	—	Battalion Route march. JL	
"	3.2.16	—	Routine Work JL	
"	4.2.16	—	Routine Work JL	
"	5.2.16	—	Routine Work JL	
"	6.2.16	—	No.3 Platoon, under Lieut. H.C. GORDON proceeded to TOUTENCOURT as an Advance Party to take over JL	
"	—	—	Billets for the Battalion. JL	
"	7.2.16	—	Routine Work. JL	
TOUTENCOURT	8.2.16	—	The Battalion left CANAPLES at 10a.m. and marched to TOUTENCOURT, arriving at 3.50 p.m. and was billeted there for the night. JL	
FORCEVILLE	9.2.16	—	Continued march to FORCEVILLE at 10a.m, arriving there at 12.15pm where they were billeted. JL	
"	10.2.16	—	Routine Work JL	
"	11.2.16	—	Routine Work. JL	
"	12.2.16	—	The Battalion, attached to 109th Inf. Brigade, took over the portion of the line held by 11th Bn. Royal Irish Rifles	APPENDIX No 1
"	—	—	as shewn on attached map. "A" and "C" Companies in Trenches "B" and "D" Coys in Brigade Reserve at FORCEVILLE. JL	N/AP.
FORCEVILLE and TRENCHES	13.2.16	—	11/7456 Pte J. PILE and 12/22698 Pte J. GORDON wounded. JL	
"	14.2.16	—	Situation normal JL	

Army Form C. 2118.

WAR DIARY
or
INTELLIGENCE SUMMARY.
(Erase heading not required.)

Instructions regarding War Diaries and Intelligence Summaries are contained in F. S. Regs., Part II. and the Staff Manual respectively. Title pages will be prepared in manuscript.

Place	Date	Hour	Summary of Events and Information	Remarks and references to Appendices
FORCEVILLE AND TRENCHES	15.2.16	-	Situation Normal. MK	
"	16.2.16	-	"B" and "D" Companies relieved "A" and "C" Companies in Trenches. MK	
"	17.2.16	-	Hot day. Trenches very wet and muddy. Situation Normal. MK	
"	18.2.16	-	Situation Normal. MK	
"	19.2.16	-	Situation Normal. No.17/7474 Pte W.WILLIAMS wounded at UNION JACK CLUB, AUCHONVILLERS. MK At 6p.m. an intense bombardment commenced on our LEFT and lasted until 6.45p.m. Reserve Companies were called out and "stood by" from 6pm to 10pm. "A" & "C" Companies relieved "B" & "D" Companies who proceeded to MAILLY MAILLET where they were billeted MK	
"	20.2.16	-	No.17/22706, Pte J.EVANS wounded after relief in bay near Sap head of RIGHT SECTOR	
MAILLY MAILLET AND TRENCHES	21.2.16	-	Situation Normal MK	
"	22.2.16	-	Situation Normal MK	
"	23.2.16	-	Situation Normal. Heavy fall of snow MK	
"	24.2.16	-	The portion of the Trenches the Battalion was holding was taken over by the 8th Bn R. IRISH RIFLES. "A" and "C" Companies relieved from Trenches and returned to billets at FORCEVILLE. "B" and "D" Companies returned to FORCEVILLE from MAILLY MAILLET. Men Event MK	
FORCEVILLE	25.2.16	-	Routine Work. - Cold. MK	

Army Form C. 2118.

WAR DIARY
or
INTELLIGENCE SUMMARY.

(Erase heading not required.)

Instructions regarding War Diaries and Intelligence Summaries are contained in F.S. Regs., Part II. and the Staff Manual respectively. Title pages will be prepared in manuscript.

Place	Date	Hour	Summary of Events and Information	Remarks and references to Appendices
FORCEVILLE	26.2.16	—	Routine Work. Cold.	
"	27.2.16	—	Routine Work. Thaw.	
TRENCHES	28.2.16	—	The Battalion took over the portion of the line held by 10th Bn R. Inniskilling Fus. as shown on attached map. The relief was completed at 9.55 p.m. Situation normal.	APPENDIX "2" map.
"	29.2.16	—	Situation normal. Strength of Battalion on 29.2.1916 - 31 Officers 942 Other Ranks	

29-2-1916.

C.H. Army Lieut. Col.,
Comdg. 11th (S.) Bn. R. Inniskilling Fus.

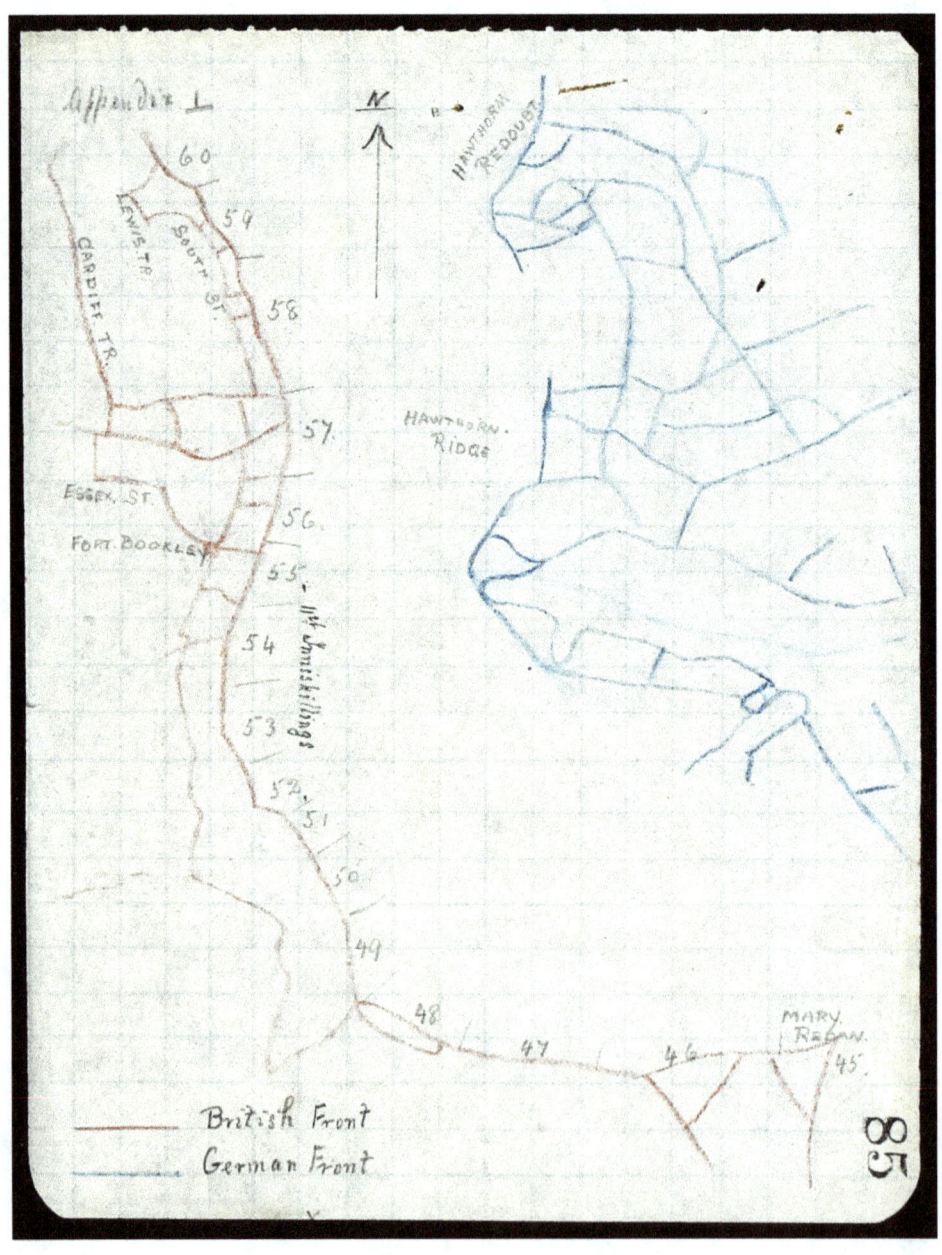

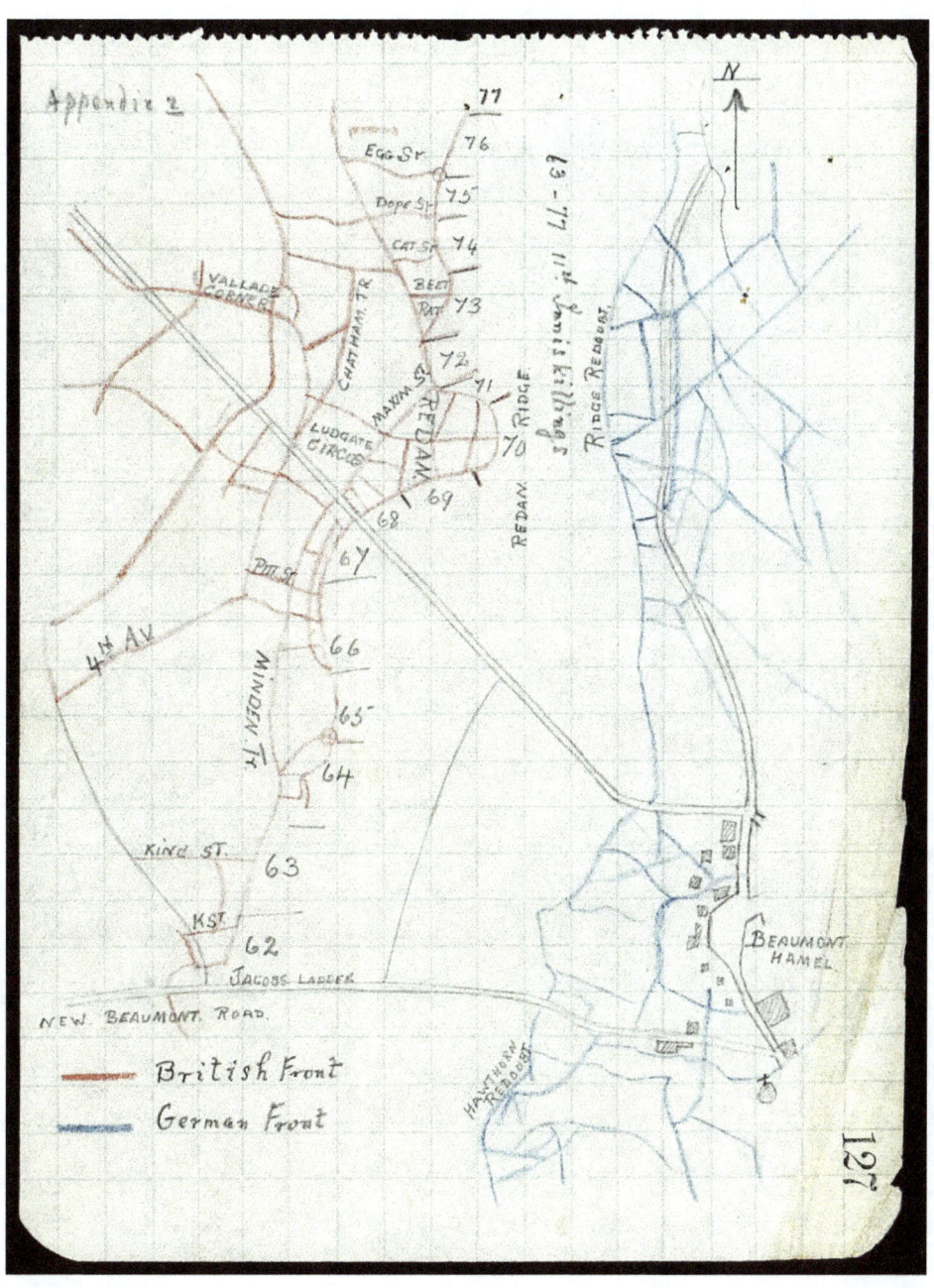

ORIGINAL

$\frac{109}{36}$

CONFIDENTIAL.

WAR DIARY

of

11th. (S.) Bn. Rl. INNISKILLING FUSILIERS.

From 1st March, 1916   To 31st March, 1916.

(Volume No. 6)

Army Form C. 2118.

WAR DIARY
or
INTELLIGENCE SUMMARY.
(Erase heading not required.)

Instructions regarding War Diaries and Intelligence Summaries are contained in F. S. Regs., Part II. and the Staff Manual respectively. Title pages will be prepared in manuscript.

Place	Date	Hour	Summary of Events and Information	Remarks and references to Appendices
TRENCHES	1/3/16	—	Situation Normal. Artillery fire at intervals during day and night.	
"	2/3/16	—	Same as for 1/3/16. Enemy exploded mine about 11.30pm in front of REDAN.	
FORCEVILLE	3/3/16	—	Situation Normal. Relieved by 15th Royal Irish Rifles at 11pm. and returned to Rest Billets at FORCEVILLE.	
"	4/3/16	—	Orders received that the Battalion was to proceed to MESNIL on the 5th inst., in support of the 12th Rs. Irish Rifles and be attached to 108th Brigade.	
MESNIL	5/3/16	—	Marched from FORCEVILLE at 1.30pm via HERAUVILLE - ENGLEBELMER - MARTINSART to MESNIL and took over billets from 9th Rs. IRISH FUSILIERS. Relief completed at 5.30pm. 3 Platoons of "C" Company took over at NOUNO KEEP.	
"	6/3/16	—	Situation Normal.	
TRENCHES	7/3/16	—	Took over the portion of the Trenches held by 12th Rs. IRISH RIFLES. Relief completed at 8.30pm. Situation Normal.	
"	8/3/16	—	Situation Normal. Artillery shelled enemy transport from 7 to 9pm. Casualties. No. 11/18118 Pte. T. HICKS Accidentally wounded Rifle fire. 11/18731 Pte. E. Brown, wounded artillery fire and 11/18/34 Pte. S. MATHEWS, wounded rifle fire.	
"	9/3/16	—	Situation Normal. Enemy shelled trenches on our Right during the afternoon. Casualties 11/8361 Pte. J. GARBUTT, killed by rifle fire	
"	10/3/16	—	Situation normal during the day.	

1577 Wt. W10791/1773 500,000 1/15 D. D. & L.   A.D.S.S./Forms/C. 2118.

Army Form C. 2118.

WAR DIARY
or
INTELLIGENCE SUMMARY.
(Erase heading not required.)

Place	Date	Hour	Summary of Events and Information	Remarks and references to Appendices
TRENCHES	10/3/16		Continued 11/22883 Pte. J.R. KENNEDY wounded by rifle fire, since died. During the night the enemy's artillery (CIRCUS) heavily bombarded the sector on our Right from 11pm to 12mn.	
MESNIL	11/3/16	-	Situation Normal. Relieved by 14th R. Irish Rifles at 9.15 p.m. Returned to Rest Billets at MESNIL.	
"	12/3/16	"	Battalion Resting - Sunday	
"	13/3/16	"	Employed on R.E. Works.	
"	14/3/16	"	Employed on R.E. Works. Our artillery bombarded THIEPVAL from 12 noon to 1.30 pm in retaliation for enemy's bombardment on the 10th inst. Casualties Capt. J.E. BRYSON wounded, 14/9230 Pte. R.T. STRATTON, 11/14794 Pte. A. DEVINE, and 1/10085 Pte. R. JOHNSTON, all wounded by artillery fire.	
TRENCHES	15/3/16	-	Relieved 14th R. IRISH RIFLES in trenches at 9.30 pm Situation Normal.	
"	16/3/16	"	Situation Normal. Some shells and 25 French Mortar shells fired into the front line trench about 4.40 pm. No Casualties.	
"	17/3/16	"	Situation Normal. Front line shelled in the afternoon. Casualties 11/1864 Pte W. SMITH killed 11/13434 Pte. A. CAMPBELL wounded 11/9793 R.T. BROTHERSTONE, wounded 11/13040 Pte S. MCELWETRICK wounded, all by artillery fire	

Army Form C. 2118.

WAR DIARY
of
INTELLIGENCE SUMMARY.
(Erase heading not required.)

Instructions regarding War Diaries and Intelligence Summaries are contained in F. S. Regs., Part II. and the Staff Manual respectively. Title pages will be prepared in manuscript.

Place	Date	Hour	Summary of Events and Information	Remarks and references to Appendices
TRENCHES	18/3/16		Situation Normal. Artillery wire cutting. Fired 130 shells	
"	19/3/16		Situation Normal. Enemy shelled HAMEL at 9.40pm. Trying to open fire. G. CLARKE wounded	
"	20/3/16		17/20981. Pte. C. PEOPLES wounded. Lid Artillery fire.	
"	21/3/16		Situation Normal. Enemy fired 30 Trench Mortar Shells in the afternoon. Knocked in our Communication Trench.	
MESNIL	22/3/16		Situation normal. Relieved by 14th R. IRISH RIFLES at 9pm. Returned to Rest billets at MESNIL. "D" Company less 1 Platoon to MOUND KEEP. Battalion resting	
"	23/3/16		Battalion employed on R.E. Works.	
"	24/3/16		Same as on 23.3.16	
"	25/3/16		Same as on 24.3.16	
"	26/3/16		Same as on 25.3.16	
TRENCHES	27/3/16		Relieved 14th R. IRISH RIFLES in the trenches at 9.40pm. Situation Normal	
"	28/3/16		Situation Normal. A few "whiz-bangs" and "oil cans" came over during the day	
"	29/3/16		Situation Normal. Artillery fire in the afternoon.	
"	30/3/16		Situation Normal. 7 "Oil cans" were fired by Enemy about 6pm. No damage done	

Army Form C. 2118.

WAR DIARY
or
INTELLIGENCE SUMMARY.
(Erase heading not required.)

Instructions regarding War Diaries and Intelligence Summaries are contained in F. S. Regs., Part II. and the Staff Manual respectively. Title pages will be prepared in manuscript.

Place	Date	Hour	Summary of Events and Information	Remarks and references to Appendices
TRENCHES	31/3/16	—	Situation Normal. Enemy fired some "oil cans" about 6.30 p.m. Our artillery retaliated. Extract from 109th Infantry Brigade Order dated 31.3.16. No 17/28909. Pte. Louis Hazlett, 11th Bn. R. Inniskilling Fus. has been awarded the "DISTINGUISHED CONDUCT MEDAL" for his gallantry and courage on the night of March 14, 1916 outside the REDAN, when he did excellent work towards rescuing 3 men who were entombed in a mine which had been exploded by the Germans and was full of gas. The Divisional Commander wished to add his congratulations. Strength of Battalion on 31.3.1916 :- 32 Officers 980 Other Ranks.	

Lieut Col.
Comdg. 11th (S) Bn. R. Inniskilling Fus.

O.C. 11th R. Inniskilling Fus.

I propose to send in the reliefs tomorrow in the following order if this will suit you please –

order of
march 14th –

			11th
1st	B Coy relieves		B Coy Reserve
2nd	C " "		A " Right
3rd	A " "		C " Left
4th	D " "		D " Support

D Coy 14th moves in from the MOUND not to enter HAMEL before 7.30 pm –

I am sending you representatives of Coys leaving here at 2 pm, tomorrow as last time to take over Trench stores &c – Will you kindly arrange to take over Guards &c at the MOUND –

B Coy of 14th – head of

38

Column ~~tears~~ passes
Barrier at Head of
JACOBS LADDER at
7 pm tomorrow —

~~order~~   E A Plunkett Major
                 OC 14 R Irish Rifles.
20.3.16 —

Secret

Reference Map Sheet
57 D. 1/40,000

OPERATION ORDER No. 8.
by
LIEUT. COLONEL, W.F.HESSEY,
COMMANDING, 11th.(S)Bn.Rl.INNISKILLING FUS.
21.3.16.

Copy No. 6

1. The Battalion will be relieved by the 14th. Bn. Rl. Irish Rifles on the night of 21/22nd. March, 1916.

2. Order in which Companies will be relieved will be as follows:-
   1st. Reserve Company.   Our "B" Coy. by "B" Coy. 14. R.I.R.
   2nd. Right Front   "   " "A" " " "C" "   "
   3rd. Left Front,   "   " "C" " " "A" "   "
   4th. Support   "   " "D" " " "D" "   "

3. Guides from Companies to meet the relieving Companies of 14th. Rl. Irish Rifles to be at the Guard Post where road from MESNIL enters HAMEL at 7 p.m. (Not shown on Map)

4. Companies on relief, to march by Platoons to Billets at MESNIL, except "D" Company (1 platoon for MESNIL) which marches to MOUND KEEP and AVELUY WOOD.

5. Representatives from Companies to take over billets, stores, also 1 cook per Company, signallers etc., to be sent back to MESNIL via JACOBS LADDER or in the case of "D" Company, via MOUND KEEP, not later than 4 p.m. this afternoon.
   1 Platoon of "D" Company will take over Guards at MESNIL at earliest opportunity.

6. Trench Stores to be handed over & lists forwarded to the Adjutant by 10 a.m. 22nd instant.

7. Each Company will make arrangements with the relieving Company to take over the work in hand.

8. Completion of relief to be notified by wire or runner to Battalion Headquarters in trenches.

   Completion of relief at MOUND KEEP to be notified to Battalion Headquarters in Billets.

(Sd)W.Moore, Capt.,
Adjt, 11th.(S)Bn.Rl.Inniskilling Fusrs.

Copy No. 1.   To ....
 "   " 2.   To ....
 "   " 3.   To ....
 "   " 4.   To ....
 "   " 5.   To ....
 "   " 6.   To 14th Rl Innis Rifles
 "   " 7.   To
 "   " 8.   To

Reference Map
Sheet No. 57D
1/40,000.

Copy No. 2

S 107A

Secret

Operation Order No. 9.
by
LIEUT-COL. W. F. HESSEY.
Comdg. 11th (S) Bn. Rl. Inniskilling Fusiliers.
27. 3. 16.

1. The Battalion will relieve the 14th Bn. Rl. Irish Rifles. in the Left Sub Sector on the night 27/28th March 1916.

2. The order of relief will be as follows:-
   1st. Reserve Company.   Our "A" Coy. relieves "B" Coy. R.Ir.R.
   2nd. Right Front   "   "   "D"   "   "   "C" "   "
   3rd. Left Front   "   "   "B"   "   "   "A" "   "
   4th. Support   "   "C"   "   "   "D" "   "

   "A" Coy. Starts from Barrier MESNIL with No.16 Platoon, 7 p.m.
   "D" "   Enters HAMEL from MOUND KEEP.   7.20 p.m.
   "B" "   Starts from Barrier MESNIL"   7.25 p.m.
   "C" "   Follows "B" Coy.

   100 yards between platoons, 200 yards between Companies. Platoons to march in single file

3. Guides from the 14th R. Irish Rifles will meet our Coys at the Guard Post where MESNIL Road enters HAMEL (not shown on map.)

4. Each Coy will send on 1 Officer and 1 N.C.O. to take over Trench Stores, etc., to arrive in trenches not later than 4 p.m.

   Signalling Sergeant and Signallers to arrive in trenches 4 p.m.

   Representatives from each Coy to be left behind to hand over billets if they are not handed over before Coy. marches off.

5. All billets and surroundings to be left as clean as possible and all rubbish collected and placed on incinerator.

6. "D" Coy. at MOUND KEEP - AVELUY WOOD - and McMAHONS POST - will be relieved by parties from the 14th. R. Irish Rifles in time to proceed.
   "D" Coy. will leave 1 Sergt, 1 Corpl. and 19 men at MOUND KEEP to assist the R.E. with the work of making dug-outs, propping, etc.
   This party will be attached to O.C. Coy, 14th R. Irish Rifles for discipline, not for rations.

7. Trench Stores to be taken over and lists sent to Adjutant by 10 a.m. 28th inst.

8. Completion of relief to be notified to Battalion Headquarters in trenches by wire or runner.

(Sd) W. Moore,   Capt.
Adjt, 11th (S) Bn. Rl. Inniskilling Fusiliers.

Copy No.1
  "   " 2
  "   " 3

Dictated to "A" Coy at 1.30 p.m.
   "   " "B" "   "   "   "
   "   " "C" "   "   "   "
   "   " "D" "   "   "   "

CONFIDENTIAL.

WAR DIARY

OF

11th.(SERVICE) BATTALION ROYAL INNISKILLING FUSRS.

From - 1st. April, 1916, To - 30th. April, 1916.

(Volume No. 7.)

Army Form C. 2118.

WAR DIARY
or
INTELLIGENCE SUMMARY.
(Erase heading not required.)

Instructions regarding War Diaries and Intelligence Summaries are contained in F.S. Regs., Part II. and the Staff Manual respectively. Title pages will be prepared in manuscript.

Place	Date	Hour	Summary of Events and Information	Remarks and references to Appendices
TRENCHES.	1.4.16		Situation normal.	
" "	2.4.16		Situation normal. At 4.30 pm Nº 19/3767 Pte. A. Murray dropped a Mills Grenade into a shelter at STONEBRIDGE (Q24.a.5.2) causing the following casualties:- KILLED - 13476 Pte W. Clark, wounded since died, 17284 Pte J. Armstrong. WOUNDED - 22962 Pte. C. Doherty - 22650 Pte R. Eaton - 17231 Pte 119 Fleming - 16211 Pte J. McCrea. 16834 Pte. S. Holywell wounded by M.G. fire. The Battalion was relieved by the 14th Rl Irish Rifles and returned to Rest Billets at MESNIL.	
MESNIL	3.4.16		Enemy shelled MESNIL during the day. At about 4.10 p.m. the undernamed were killed and wounded by one shell. 17392 Pte N. McFarren, 22468 Pte J. Gillan, 19933 Pte R. McConnell, 23167 Pte H. McRoy. WOUNDED. 1 killed and 11 wounded of 9th Rl Irish Fusiliers, and 1 man R.F.A wounded. Total Casualties 1 killed - 16 wounded.	
" "	4.4.16		Battalion employed on R.E. Work.	
" "	5.4.16		Battalion employed on R.E. Work.	
" "	6.4.16		Battalion employed on R.E. Work. MESNIL heavily shelled by enemy from 8.45 pm to 10.15 pm. No casualties. Some damage done to the houses in village.	

Army Form C. 2118.

WAR DIARY
or
INTELLIGENCE SUMMARY.
(Erase heading not required.)

Instructions regarding War Diaries and Intelligence Summaries are contained in F. S. Regs., Part II. and the Staff Manual respectively. Title pages will be prepared in manuscript.

Place	Date	Hour	Summary of Events and Information	Remarks and references to Appendices
MESNIL	7.4.16		Battalion employed on R.E. Work.	
"	8.4.16		Relieved 1st R. Irish Rifles in trenches. Relief completed 9.15 pm.	
TRENCHES	9.4.16		Situation Normal.	
"	10.4.16		Situation Normal. No. 11/20373, C.S.M. Hunt J. "D" Coy wounded by rifle fire.	
"	11.4.16		Situation Normal. No. 11935 Lance Corpl. J. Hindenos, killed by artillery fire at O.23.a.4.0.	
"	12.4.16		Situation Normal.	
"	13.4.16		Situation Normal. No. 11090 Pte. Nelanophy J. and 17/2881 Pte. W.J. Briggs, both wounded by shell fire.	
"	14.4.16		Situation Normal. Relieved by 15th R. Irish Rifles at 9.40 pm and returned to billets at MESNIL. "A" Coy at YOUNG KEEP. Lieut. Col. W.J. HESSEY took over Command of 109th Inf. Bde. during the temporary absence of Brig. Gen. T.E. HICKMAN, and Command of the Battalion devolved on Capt. W.T. SEWELL.	
MESNIL	15.4.16		Situation Normal. No. 11094 Pte. D.M Laughlan and 11904 Pte. R. Derby wounded in MESNIL by Machine Gun fire. Capt. The Earl of Leitrim	

WAR DIARY
or
INTELLIGENCE SUMMARY.

Army Form C. 2118.

Place	Date	Hour	Summary of Events and Information	Remarks and references to Appendices
MESNIL	15.4.16		rejoined from leave and took over Command of the Battalion during the temporary absence of Lieut. Col. W.J. Woodey.	
"	16.4.16		Situation normal. Battalion employed on R.E. work.	
"	17.4.16		Situation normal. 19925 L.Cpl. W.E. Ellis and 18669 Pte. J. Watson both wounded by M.G. fire on MESNIL-HAMEL road.	
"	18.4.16		Situation normal. 19870 Pte. F. Crooke wounded by M.G. fire on HAMEL-MESNIL road.	
"	19.4.16		Situation normal.	
"	20.4.16		The Battalion moved from MESNIL and MOUND KEEP as follows:- "A" Company to SOUTH ANTRIM VILLAS. "C" Coy to AUTHUILE. "B" and "D" Coys and Headquarters to huts in MARTINSART WOOD. Casualties No.14/14246 Pte. G. Mumford wounded by rifle fire at MILL BRIDGE. AUTHUILE	
MARTINSART Wood etc.	21.4.16		Situation normal	
"	22.4.16		Situation normal	
"	23.4.16		Situation normal. Casualty - 14024 Pte. N. Booth wounded by artillery at SOUTH ANTRIM VILLAS.	

WAR DIARY
or
INTELLIGENCE SUMMARY.
(Erase heading not required.)

Army Form C. 2118.

Place	Date	Hour	Summary of Events and Information	Remarks and references to Appendices
MARTINSART Wood	24.4.16		Situation normal. Battalion relieved 9th Bn. Rl. Irish. Rif. in Right Sub Sector. 3 Platoons per Company in Front Line, and 1 Platoon per Company in Reserve at GORDON CASTLE.	
TRENCHES	25.4.16		Situation normal. Casualty No. 1. Sept. J. McCann wounded + artillery fire.	
"	26.4.16		Situation normal. Casualties. 17273 Pte. F. McKelvie and 13820 Pte. J. Adams wounded by Artillery fire. THIEPVAL.	
"	27.4.16		Situation normal. Casualty No. 1. Pte. G. McGowan, wounded, since died. Artillery fire.	
"	28.4.16		Situation normal.	
"	29.4.16		Situation normal. Casualty 2nd Lieut. P.H. Hall wounded, rifle fire.	
"	30.4.16		Situation normal. Battalion relieved by 14th Rl. Irish Rifles. Moved into Rest Billets as follows. Headquarters A + C Coy. to Huts in MARTINSART WOOD. B Coy. into tents in MARTINSART WOOD. D Coy. into Billets in MARTINSART.	

Strength of Battalion on 30.4.16. Officers 33. Other Ranks 967.

W. Hughes Capt.
Comdg. 14th (S) Bn. R. Innis. Fus.

CONFIDENTIAL.

WAR DIARY

of

11th. (SERVICE) BATTALION ROYAL INNISKILLING FUSILIERS,

From .... 1st. MAY, 1916. to .... 31st. MAY, 1916.

(Volume No. 8.)

WAR DIARY
or
INTELLIGENCE SUMMARY.
(Erase heading not required.)

Army Form C. 2118.

Instructions regarding War Diaries and Intelligence Summaries are contained in F. S. Regs., Part II. and the Staff Manual respectively. Title pages will be prepared in manuscript.

Place	Date	Hour	Summary of Events and Information	Remarks and references to Appendices
MARTINSART WOOD	1.5.16		Situation normal.	
MARTINSART WOOD	2.5.16		Situation normal.	
"	3.5.16		Situation normal.	
"	4.5.16		Situation normal.	
"	5.5.16		Situation normal. A few shells dropped on outskirts of Wood. No damage.	
"	6.5.16		Situation normal.	
"	7.5.16		Battalion changed station. Relieved by 13th Bn. R. Irish Rifles. The Battalion marched to VARENNES via HEDAUVILLE, arriving at 12.10 pm and relieving 15th R. Irish Rifles.	
VARENNES	8.5.16		Situation normal.	
"	9.5.16		Situation normal.	
"	10.5.16		Situation normal. Battalion at Divisional Baseville Trenches practising attack in afternoon.	
"	11.5.16		Battalion on Divisional Exercise.	
"	12.5.16		Battalion at Divisional Exercise.	

1577 Wt.W10791/1773 500,000 1/15 D. D. & L. A.D.S.S./Forms/C. 2118.

Army Form C. 2118.

WAR DIARY
or
INTELLIGENCE SUMMARY.
(Erase heading not required.)

Instructions regarding War Diaries and Intelligence Summaries are contained in F. S. Regs., Part II. and the Staff Manual respectively. Title pages will be prepared in manuscript.

Place	Date	Hour	Summary of Events and Information	Remarks and references to Appendices
VARENNES	13.5.16		Operations on Dummy Trenches postponed on account of Rain. Battalion Route Marching.	
-o-	14.5.16		Sunday. Divine Service. Lieut Col. W.F. HESSEY arrived from Eversburg, 109th Infantry Brigade and took over command of the Battalion	
-o-	15.5.16		Operation on Dummy Trenches postponed on account of Rain.	
-o-	16.5.16		Operations on Dummy Trenches in afternoon. Company Training in morning.	
-o-	17.5.16		Operations on Dummy Trenches.	
-o-	18.5.16		Operations on Dummy Trenches.	
-o-	19.5.16		Brigade Operations at Dummy Trenches in morning. Officers - Recreation	
-o-	20.5.16		Company Training and Working Parties for R.E.s. Major THE EARL OF LEITRIM admitted to Div REST STATION.	
-o-	21.5.16		Sunday. Divine Service in morning. Company Training in afternoon. Working Parties for R.E.	
-o-	22.5.16		Company Training and Working Parties for R.E.	
-o-	23.5.16		Brigade Day at Dummy Trenches.	
-o-	24.5.16		Operations at Dummy Trenches and Working Parties for R.E.s	

Army Form C. 2118.

WAR DIARY
or
INTELLIGENCE SUMMARY.
(Erase heading not required.)

Instructions regarding War Diaries and Intelligence Summaries are contained in F. S. Regs., Part II. and the Staff Manual respectively. Title pages will be prepared in manuscript.

Place	Date	Hour	Summary of Events and Information	Remarks and references to Appendices
WARENNES	25.5.16		Operations on Dummy Trenches and Working Parties for R.E.s. Capt. W.T. Sewell took over command of the Battalion during the absence on leave of Lieut. Col. W.F. Hessey. Days of 61 officers.	
-//-	26.5.16		Brigade Operations on Dummy Trenches and Working Parties for R.E.s.	
-//-	27.5.16		Stokes Mortar Demonstration on Dummy Trenches and Working Parties for R.E.s. Afternoon Brigade Sports.	
-//-	28.5.16		Sunday. Divine Service and Working Parties for R.E.	
-//-	29.5.16		Brigade Operations on Dummy Trenches and Working Parties for R.E.	
-//-	30.5.16		Company Training & Working Parties. Operations on Dummy Trenches postponed on account of Rain.	
-//-	31.5.16		Battalion Operations on Dummy Trenches in afternoon. Company Training in afternoon. Strength of Battalion on 31.5.16: 33 Officers 1034 Other Ranks.	

W. Sewell. Capt.
Comdg. 11th (S) Bn. R. Sussex Regt.

109th Brigade.
36th Division.

1/11th BATTALION

ROYAL INNISKILLING FUSILIERS

JUNE 1916

WAR DIARY
or
INTELLIGENCE SUMMARY

(Erase heading not required.)

Army Form C. 2118.

Instructions regarding War Diaries and Intelligence Summaries are contained in F. S. Regs., Part II. and the Staff Manual respectively. Title Pages will be prepared in manuscript.

Place	Date	Hour	Summary of Events and Information	Remarks and references to Appendices
VARENNES	1.6.16.		Situation Normal. Battalion training under Company arrangements.	Appendix No 1.
"	2.6.16.		Situation normal. 3 Companies on working parties for R.E.,	Congratulations from G.O.C. Div. and Brigade
"	3.6.16.		Situation Normal. Same as on 2nd. June.	
"	4.6.16.		Early morning parades began. Divine Service, also Working Parties.	
"	5.6.16.		Brigade Operations on Practice Trenches at CLAIRFAYE, also Working Parties. Lieut. Col. W.F.HESSEY, rejoined from Leave of absence and assumed Command of the Battalion.	
"	6.6.16.		Company Training and Working Parties.	
"	7.6.16.		Brigade Operations on Corps Training Ground at BAIZIEUX; also Working Parties.	
"	8.6.16.		Divisional Operations at CLAIRFAYE Practice Trenches, also Working Parties.	
"	9.6.16.		Divisional Concentration Operations at BAIZIEUX, and Working Parties. Lieut. Col. W.F.Hessey, relinquished Command of the Battalion on appointment to Command 110th. Infantry Brigade, and Command of Battalion devolved on Captain J.S.Myles.	
"	10.6.16-11.6.16.		Divisional Operations at BAIZIEUX; also Working Parties.	
"	12.6.16.		Sunday - Divine Service. Brigade Operations at CLAIRFAYE Practice Trenches ; also Working Parties. Major G.H.BRUSH (10th.Bn.R.Innis.Fus) joined the Battalion on appointment to Temporary Command and took over from Capt. J.S.Myles. Rev. A. Spence, C.F., attached to Battalion from this date and joined.	
"	13.6.16.		Company Training and Working Parties.	
"	14.6.16.		Company Training and Working Parties. Time advanced 1 hour at 11 p.m.	
"	15.6.16.		Divisional exercise at BAIZIEUX; also Working Parties.	
"	16.6.16.		Battalion moved from VARENNES to AVELUY WOOD, arriving there at 7.45 p.m.	
AVELUY WOOD	17.6.16		Battalion on Working Parties. Casualties :- 14034, Pte. H. Carruthers and 22680, Pte. R. Eades, "A" Coy. wounded by Artillery Fire at S.W. corner of THIEPVAL WOOD.	

Army Form C. 2118.

WAR DIARY
or
INTELLIGENCE SUMMARY

(Erase heading not required.)

Instructions regarding War Diaries and Intelligence Summaries are contained in F. S. Regs., Part II. and the Staff Manual respectively. Title Pages will be prepared in manuscript.

Place	Date	Hour	Summary of Events and Information	Remarks and references to Appendices
AVELUY WOOD	18.6.16.		Battalion on Working Parties. Casualties "C" Company - 18658, Corpl. G. Hutchinson, 13395, Pte. J. Cochrane, 24200, Pte. Spiers, W. 24799, Pte. R. McDonald - all wounded by Artillery Fire, at S.W. corner of THIEPVAL WOOD. Orders received that both Brigade would attack after bombardment of the German lines which was to last for 6 days. These they were lettered T. U. V. W. X. Y. & Z day. attack was to begin	
"	19.6.16.		Battalion on Working Parties.	
"	20.6.16.		Same as yesterday.	
"	21.6.16.		Same as yesterday - Casualties "A" Coy. 18311, Pte. A. Wilson and 25954, Pte. T. Murray, both Shell Shock, S.W. corner of THIEPVAL WOOD.	
"	22.6.16.		Battalion on Working Parties.	
"	23.6.16.		"T" Day. Battalion moved from AVELUY WOOD to FORCEVILLE. 1st. platoon left at 6.30 p.m. Battalion took over Huts at FORCEVILLE at 9.0 p.m.	
FORCEVILLE	24.6.16.		"U" Day. Bombardment by Artillery began.	
"	25.6.16.		"V" Day. Sunday - Divine Service. Artillery Bombarding heavily.	
"	26.6.16.		"W" Day. Artillery still bombarding German Lines heavily.	
"	27.6.16.		"X" Day. Artillery still bombarding. Battalion moved to MARTINSART, leaving FORCEVILLE (1st. Platoon) at 9.30 p.m., and arrived at MARTINSART (last platoon) at 11.50 p.m. Heavy bombardment continuing. Enemy retaliated with about 20 shells on MARTINSART.	
MARTINSART	28.6.16.		"Y" Day. Bombardment still continuing. Battalion left MARTINSART at 9 p.m. for THIEPVAL WOOD to relieve 5th.Bn.R.Innis.Fus., arrived and relief completed at 11.50 p.m. & went line handed to Bn. was Instructions received that Advance was postponed, and lettering of days altered accordingly: "Z" day being numbered "Y1" day, following day "Y11" day and following day "Z" day, on which the attack would be launched.	

NOTE.

Army Form C. 2118.

WAR DIARY
or
INTELLIGENCE SUMMARY
(Erase heading not required.)

Instructions regarding War Diaries and Intelligence Summaries are contained in F. S. Regs., Part II. and the Staff Manual respectively. Title Pages will be prepared in manuscript.

Place	Date	Hour	Summary of Events and Information	Remarks and references to Appendices
TRENCHES THIEPVAL WOOD.	29.6.16.		"Y1" day. Bombardment continuing heavily. Enemy retaliating on our Front Line and GORDON CASTLE. Enemy sent over many "Tear" shells in the neighbourhood of GORDON CASTLE. Casualties to 12 noon - 14136, L.Sgt.T.Willis, 20905, Pte. J. McMaster, Shell Shock, 17282, Pte. Simpson, J. and 18379, Pte. Stewart, J. Killed, 18670, L.Cp. W. Richardson, 23187, Pte. H. McIlroy and 15243, Pte. Jack White, wounded, all Artillery Fire, THIEPVAL WOOD.	
"	30.6.16.		"Y11" day. Heavy Bombardment continued. Enemy retaliated on our Front Line, also GORDON CASTLE. Casualties, reported at 12 noon - Killed, 2. Wounded, 5, Shell Shock, 5. Strength of the Battalion on this day; :- 38 Officers, and 991. Other Ranks. [signature] Lieut.Col., Comdg,11th.(S)Bn.Rl.Inniskilling Fuslrs., 30th.June,1916.	

APPENDIX 1.

War Diary, for month June, 1916.

The following is a copy of a letter received by the Commanding Officer from Major General O.S. Nugent, Commanding 36th. Division, on the 24.6.16.:-

"H.Q. 36th.Divn.
June,23.1916.

"I wish to thank your Battalion through you for the
"way in which they have worked during the past weeks.
"From my own observation and from reports received
"from all sources, I think that Officers and men
"deserve the highest credit for the good honest work
"they have put in. Where all have worked well itxmay
"as has been the case, it may seem invidious to select
"one particular Battalion for special praise, but the
"11th.Rl.Innis.Fus have earned it from everyone who has
"worked with them.
"Will you please thank the Battalion from me and tell
"them that I wish them the best of luck.
Yours sincerely,
(Sd) Oliver Nugent.

The following is a copy of a congratulatory letter received from G.O.C. 36th. Division through official channels,:-

"The G.O.C. wishes to express his great satisfaction
"with the good work performed by the 11th.R.Innis.Fus.
"Parties from this Battalion were found for work on
"the shelters of the newly arrived French Batteries,
"also for assisting the Tunnellers in THIEPVAL WOOD and
"for carrying up R.E., stores.
"From all three sources reports were received as to the
"exceptionally good and hard work performed by this
"Battalion.
"Success in trench warfare is so largely dependant upon
"hard work in connection with the preparations for the
"offensive that it is difficult to exagerate the value of
"really good work done in this respect.
"Please inform the C.O. of the Battalion of the contents
"of this letter.

....

The Brigadier General in forarding the above letter of
"commendation from the G.O.C. Division wishes to offer
"his personal congratulations to you and all ranks of the
"Battalion on the good reports earned by its working
"parties.
"The Brigadier would like you to let all Ranks know of
"the Divisional Commander's appreciation of their good
"work."

109th Brigade.
36th Division.

1/11th BATTALION

ROYAL INNISKILLING FUSILIERS

JULY 1916

Army Form C. 2118.

WAR DIARY
or
INTELLIGENCE SUMMARY.
(Erase heading not required.)

Instructions regarding War Diaries and Intelligence Summaries are contained in F.S. Regs., Part II. and the Staff Manual respectively. Title pages will be prepared in manuscript.

Place	Date	Hour	Summary of Events and Information	Remarks and references to Appendices
			Map Reference France. LENS II. 1/100,000 and 57D. S.E. 1 and 2. (parts of) Trench map.	
THIEPVAL WOOD	1-7-16		"Z" DAY. At 6.30 a.m. an intense bombardment commenced. At 10 minutes to Zero time the Battalion moved up in support of the 9th R.I. Inniskilling Fusiliers. At Zero time the Battalion went over the parapet, "A" Company suffered severely as they were getting out from Machine gun fire from THIEPVAL. The remaining companies on reaching the German wire came under machine gun fire from the same direction. As far as can be ascertained up to the present we have suffered severely. 7 Officers being reported wounded. Signallers and telephones were knocked out almost as soon as they crossed the parapet. 4 Scouts and 4 Runners were afterwards sent out at intervals to try and get in touch with the Battalion, 2 of these were returned wounded, the remainder were not able to pass the Barrage. Extra Signallers were sent out but did not return. "D" Coy reached their objective (THE CRUCIFIX) and remain there, the remainder of the Battalion is distributed in "C" line." The above is a copy of situation report forwarded to Bde H.Q on the first at 9.25 h.m. Total casualties were estimated at 600. fh.	Appendices 1. Map showing position of Battalion preparing to attack. Appendix 2. Map showing position of Battalion and Brigade orders sent objectives during attack. Appendix 3. Commanding Officers report on operation. Appendix 4. Congratulatory orders by G.O.C. 109th Bde 36th Division, X Corps and Belfast City Council

Army Form C. 2118.

WAR DIARY
or
INTELLIGENCE SUMMARY.
(Erase heading not required.)

Place	Date	Hour	Summary of Events and Information	Remarks and references to Appendices
THIEPVAL WOOD	2-7-16		Battalion received orders to move back out of the line and return to MARTINSART WOOD. The Battalion went into the line 21 Officers and 828 Other Ranks strong.	
MARTINSART WOOD	3-7-16		Arrived MARTINSART WOOD 4 a.m. Battalion received orders to move back to HEDAUVILLE. Moved off at 2.30 p.m. and	
HEDAUVILLE		4.30 p.m	arrived in HEDAUVILLE at 4.30 p.m Casualties estimated at Killed Other Ranks Officers 46 1 Died of Wounds 2 Wounded 335 9 Missing & Killed 6 Missing & Wounded 9 2 Missing 179 3 Total 577 15 Strength of Coys in Other Ranks coming out of trenches. A Coy 53 B " 83 C " 61 D " 54 TOTAL 251	

Army Form C. 2118.

WAR DIARY
or
INTELLIGENCE SUMMARY.
(Erase heading not required.)

Instructions regarding War Diaries and Intelligence Summaries are contained in F. S. Regs., Part II. and the Staff Manual respectively. Title pages will be prepared in manuscript.

Place	Date	Hour	Summary of Events and Information	Remarks and references to Appendices
HEDAUVILLE	4.7.16		Battalion resting in HEDAUVILLE.	
	5.7.16		Orders received to move back to HERISART. Battalion left HEDAUVILLE at 2.30 p.m. marching via VARENNES - HARPONVILLE - TOUTENCOURT to HERISART arriving at 5.40 p.m.	
HERISART	6.7.16		Battalion employed sorting kits	
	7.7.16		Orders to be ready to move off with one hours notice, taking stores as per mobilization table only.	
	8.7.16		Still awaiting orders to move. Routine work	
	9.7.16		Awaiting orders to move. Routine work	
FIENVILLERS	10.7.16		Battalion moved from HERISART to FIENVILLERS leaving 7 a.m. arriving at 2 p.m.	
CONTEVILLE	11.7.16		Moved from FIENVILLERS to CONTEVILLE leaving at 2 p.m. and arriving at 6 p.m. Battalion entrained and left at 8.47 p.m., detrained at BERGUETTE at 2.30 a.m. 12th.	Map Reference, HAZEBROOKE 5A, 1/100,000 and Belgium and France Sheet 28.S.W (Trench map)
BERGUETTE	12.7.16		Arrived at BERGUETTE at 2.30 a.m. and marched to RACQUINGHEM arriving at 8 a.m.	
RACQUINGHEM			Battalion billeted there for the night	
	13.7.16		Battalion left RACQUINGHEM at 10.15 a.m. and marched to SETQUES arriving at 4.40 p.m.	
SETQUES				

Army Form C. 2118.

WAR DIARY
or
INTELLIGENCE SUMMARY.
(Erase heading not required.)

Instructions regarding War Diaries and Intelligence Summaries are contained in F. S. Regs., Part II and the Staff Manual respectively. Title pages will be prepared in manuscript.

Place	Date	Hour	Summary of Events and Information	Remarks and references to Appendices
SETQUES	14-7-16		Cleaning billets and surroundings M.	
	15-7-16		Ordinary Training M.	
	16-7-16		Divine Service	
	17-7-16		Ordinary Training M.	
	18-7-16		Ordinary Training M.	
	19-7-16		Ordinary Training M.	
	20-7-16		Ordinary Training. Draft of 6 Officers joined. Capt J.E. Knott. DSO, Capt T.C. Hundley, 2nd Lieuts. A.G. O'Ball, J. Curley, J.A. Johnston and H. Halseed M.	
	21-7-16		Battalion left SETQUES at 8.15 a.m and marched via QUELMES-MOULLE and WATTEN to BOLLEZEELE arriving at 6 p.m M.	
BOLLEZEELE	22-7-16		Awaiting orders to move. Routine Work M.	
	23-7-16	Forenoon	Divine Service. Battalion left BOLLEZEELE in motor Busses and lorries at 1.45 p.m and arrived at ROMARIN at 7.20 p.m and marched to RED LODGE in the BOIS DE PLOEGSTEERT, where	
BOIS DE PLOEGSTEERT			Battalion relieved the 9th R. Inst. Rifles in reserve to the 108th Brigade. Relief was completed at 10.55 p.m Situation normal M.	

Army Form C. 2118.

WAR DIARY
or
INTELLIGENCE SUMMARY.
(Erase heading not required.)

Instructions regarding War Diaries and Intelligence Summaries are contained in F. S. Regs., Part II. and the Staff Manual respectively. Title pages will be prepared in manuscript.

Place	Date	Hour	Summary of Events and Information	Remarks and references to Appendices
BOIS DE PLEOGSTEERT	24.7.16		Battalion in reserve. Situation normal. Ol.	
	25.7.16		Battalion in reserve. Situation normal. Draft of 6 Officers joined 2nd Lieuts. J.G. Robertson, W.E. Hewitt, T.H. Bown, E.M. Wilkinson, J.W. O'Brien and E.W. Faulks. Ol.	
	26.7.16		Battalion in reserve, Gas alarm 11 p.m., stand down 12 p.m. Situation normal. Ol.	
	27.7.16		Battalion in reserve. Situation normal. Ol.	
	28.7.16		Battalion in reserve. Gas alarm 1 a.m. stand down 2 p.m. Situation normal. Battalion relieved 11th Bn R.W. Kent Regiment in trenches from PLOEGSTEERT—MESSINES Road inclusive to the DOUVE including 8 Bays in WINTER TRENCH. Strength in trenches 1 Platoon each Coy of 35 R.L.B.s and men exclusive of Lewis Gun teams. Battalion Headquarters and Details at HILL 63. Relief commenced 10 p.m. and completed at 1.20 a.m. 29th inst. Ol.	
	29.7.16		Situation normal. Draft of 1 Officer, 2nd Lieut. C.H. McComb and 5 men Ol.	
	30.7.16		Situation normal.	
	31.7.16		Situation normal. Strength of Battalion 31st July 38 Officers 417 Other Ranks	

1577 Wt.W10791/1773 500,000 1/15 D.D.&L. A.D.S.S./Forms/C. 2118.

War Diary, 11th (S) Bn. Rl. Innis. Fusiliers

Appendix 1
Map showing position
of battalion preparatory
to attack.

CONFIDENTIAL.

War Diary
Appendix 3.

REPORT FROM THE OFFICER COMMANDING, 11th (S)Bn.Rl.
INNISKILLING FUSILIERS, re Operations
27th June - to July, 1916.

Tuesday, 27th. June.
On the evening of the 27th. June, the Battalion left FORCEVILLE and were billeted in MARTINSART for the night 27/28th. June. As the Battalion entered the town, there was some shelling which continued during the night, but without casualties.

Wednesday, 28th June.
On the 28th. June, the Battalion moved up to THIEPVAL WOOD and took over the Sector of trenches held by the 9th. Batt. Royal Inniskilling Fusiliers. The relief was completed by 11.50 p.m.. Despite heavy shelling during this operation there were no casualties.

Thursday, 29th. June.
From 3 to 5 a.m. on the morning of the 29th. June there was an intense bombardment by the enemy, his fire being chiefly directed against GORDON CASTLE, the assembly trenches below GORDON CASTLE and the approaches to THIEPVAL WOOD. During the day the enemy bombardment was intermittent with bursts of Machine Gun fire from THIEPVAL village.
Throughout this bombardment the Front line was held by three double sentry posts and two Lewis Guns with reliefs in the service trench; the supporting being in WHITCHURCH STREET. The remainder of the Battalion was distributed in forward assembly trenches. These dispositions in my mind casualties.
During the day the Battalion was employed in keeping communication trenches open, repairing ramps, and improving the assembly trenches to be occupied by the battalion.
During the night 29th/30th June, the enemy continued bombarding heavily, particularly between the hours of 3 a.m and 4.30 a.m. on 30th. June.

Friday, 30th June.
Work was continued on the 30th June, on the same lines as previous day. The enemy sent over a large number of Lachrymatory shells, principally around GORDON CASTLE and back assembly trenches.
During the afternoon of 30th. June, I withdrew my Front line Company and placed them in their assembly trenches replacing them by my 4 sections of Bombers who were to go forward with the 9th.Bn.Rl.Innis.Fusrs. The remainder of the Battalion were settled at intervals during the afternoon in their assembly trenches. All material required for the Advance was distributed amongst Platoons and arrangements for the Advance completed before dawn.
During the night 30th.June/1st.July, the 9th. R.Innis. Fus. assembled in their forward assembly trenches and took over the Front Line.

During the 29th and 30th June, my casualties were 4 Killed and 15 wounded.

Saturday, 1st. July.
At 7.20 a.m. on the 1st. July the battalion left their assembly trenches and took over the trenches occupied by the 9th. R.Innis.Fus.
At 7.30 a.m. the battalion moved over the parapet "A" and "D" Companies leading.
The leading companies were at once exposed to the heavy barrage which was on our front line and also searching machine gun fire from the direction of THIEPVALL village.
These companies and those following suffered severely and most of their officers and N.C.O's were knocked out before reaching the SUNKENROAD the Battalion pushed on to the enemy "A" Line and crossed it, led by Captain W.T.SEWEL

who at this point was seen to fall whilst calling to his men to follow him. By this time only one officer, Lieut GALLAUGHER, was left and with the survivors passed on to "B" Line, some remaining there to assist in consolidating the CRUCIFIX whilst the remainder went forward under Company Sergeant Major BULLOCK to the "C" Line.

There was not a great deal of opposition encountered in entering the "B" Line, any Germans met with quickly threw up their hands.

Lieut. GALLAUGHER having barricaded the communication trenches leading to the CRUCIFIX, then starting making fire steps to shoot from. He then returned to "A" line to collect men and material. On his arrival at "A" Line he found part of it occupied by the Germans, so he arranged a bombing party and cleared the enemy out of the trenches towards his right erecting a barricade which he left in charge of a Lance Corporal and 6 men. From there he sent a message reporting the situation as he found it. This message is carried but I believe was received by the 9th. R. Innis. Fus. He then collected all the available men in "A" Trench and shell holes and took them forward to the CRUCIFIX. There were none of my battalion among them as they had evidently gone forward. Lieut. GALLAUGHER from this onwards, in conjunction with Lieut. McKINLEY 9th. R. Innis. Fus. worked under the orders of Major PEACOCK of the 9th. R.Innis.Fus. until they were forced to withdraw about 9.30 p.m.

The Signallers who went forward with the Battalion with telephones etc. were almost immediately knocked out and during the day I tried continually to get into touch with the battalion by runners, scouts and signallers but all were wounded except one.

During the afternoon there was some confusion owing to troops retiring from our left. This at one time appeared serious and our front line was not occupied, but owing to the energy of Captain MOORE, Lieut. GORDON and R.S.M. G. BLEAKLEY of this battalion together with Captain MULHOLLAND of the 14th. Rl. Irish Rifles, this situation was soon got in hand, these men being placed in the assembly trenches. The situation at this time was very difficult to understand and many German prisoners were mixed up with these men and many more Germans coming over the parapet. R.S.M. Bleakley at once organised a party and occupied our front line and things quickly resumed a normal aspect.

Lieut. GORDON and R.S.M. BLEAKLEY gave me very great assistance during the day. Both of these organised parties for ammunition and water and succeeded in getting water accross to the enemy "A" Line Lieut. GORDON also arranged carrying parties for wounded and during the early morning of 2nd. July, with the assistance of C.Q.M.Sgt. T. Johnston brought up rations for the battalion to the assembly trenches.

Capt. MOORE and R.S.M. BLEAKLEY were invaluable in controlling the traffic in the ELGIN AVENUE, the control system having completely broken down. This Officer and Warrant Officer stood on the parapet for hours making the supporting battalions coming up get out of this trench into the open to clear the way for the continuous stream of wounded who were now being carried down.

Lieut. KNIGHT, the Battalion Bombing Officer also rendered much assistance regulating the supply of bombs and clearing the communication trenches.

Privates Hunter and Smith, Headquarters Orderlies were invaluable and never failed in delivering their messages.

I wish to specially bring to notice the devotion to duty and the excellent work done by Capt. D.E.CROSBIE, R.A.M.C. under very trying circumstances. He was 5 days and 5 nights continuously at work in the Advanced Aid Post in ELGIN AV., and during this time organised several parties and went up to the front line trenches, searched there for wounded men which he brought back. About 1000 cases were dealt with at this Aid Post and each wounded man when dressed was given cocoa or soup and cigarettes. I wish also to mention the work done by the Stretcher Bearers under Capt. Crosbie.

Lieut. & Qr.Mr. J.Firth never failed us in sending up supplies of food and water as the water supply in ELGIN AVENUE had failed, the tank having been hit by a shell.

I should also like to mention Lieut. Mc.Corkell Transport Officer and Corporal Warren, Transport Corporal for the work done by them.

The Orderly Room Staff, consisting of Sergt. Beaty, Corpl. McDougall and L.Cpl. F. Kee did excellent work.

On the night of 3rd./4th. July, a party consisting of Capt. W.M.Moore, Lieut. H. Gallaugher and 20 Other ranks, volunteered to proceed to THIEPVAL WOOD and rescue wounded men from NO MAN's LAND. This party after a successful search returned safely, having rescued 28 wounded men.

On the night 4/5th. a small party under Capt. CROSBIE R.A.M.C. and Lieut. G.M.F.IRVINE and 4 Other Ranks went to THIEPVAL WOOD for the same purpose but were unable to leave the front line as an attack by our troops was imminent.

In conclusion I wish to draw your attention to the gallantry and devotion to duty of all Officers, N.C.O's and men in the Battalion under my Command during a very trying time.
This Battalion has been in the Line now for nearly 6 months and when not actually holding the front line have been supplying working parties, and even this did not seem to damp their ardour.

(Sd) G.H.BRUSH, Lieut.Col.,
Com'g. 14th.(S)Bn.R.Inniskilling Fus.

REPORT BY CAPTAIN D.E.CROSBIE, R.A.M.C.
M.O.i/c. 14th.(S) Bn.R. INNISKILLING FUSILIERS.

I took over the Regimental Aid Post at ROSS STREET and ELGIN AVENUE in THIEPVAL WOOD in conjunction with Lieut. GAVIN of the 14th. R.I.R. and Capt. PICKEN of 10th. R.INNIS.FUS. on the night of 28th. JUNE.
Nothing eventful happened until the night of 30th. JUNE, when we passed nearly 100 wounded through our hands.

My Stretcher Bearers remained with their Companies until the attack started when I gave them orders to collect any wounded they could find belonging to any unit and bring them to the nearest dressing station. This was carried out and the Stretcher Bearers working continually night and day we were relieved, bringing wounded back from the SUNKEN ROAD, No Man's Land and the Wood, under continual shell and machine gun fire.

We located many wounded men in dug-outs and holes in the front line which our Stretcher Bearers carried in. The difficulty in keeping the post clear of wounded was our great trouble as there seemed a great want of both R.A.M.C. Stretcher Bearers and Stretchers, so that on several occasions we had to resort to using the Regimental Stretcher Bearers to evacuate wounded to the collecting post which was great hardship to them. All wounded got hot cocoa or soup and cigarettes when they were dressed, for which they were very grateful.

I wish specially to mention the gallant work done by L.Corpl COOPER, Pte. MEGAGHY, Pte. TOLAND, Pte. BROWNE, Pte. ELLIOTT of "A" Coy. and Pte. WILSON of "C" Coy. Pte. ROBB "B" Coy. and Pte. FENWICK, "D" Coy.

These men worked continually, Corporal Cooper remaining in the trenches eight hours after the battalion was relieved to bring in a wounded man from the Front Line Trench.

The great assistance given by Lieut. Gavin, 14th. Rl. Ir. Rifles made it possible to cope with the enormous number of cases which were dealt with. He went on several occasions to the dug-outs in the front line and located many wounded, and although his feet and ankles were swollen with the continual standing, still continued his work.

Captain PICKEN also worked with splendid pluck and devotion.

The Orderlies and men of 14th. R.I.R. and 10th. R.In.F. in conjunction with my men gave very great assistance.

At one period the conjection the Aid Post became so great that I sent up to Colonel BRUSH to ask for assistance to evacuate wounded. He sent 2ndm Liut. HANNA who collected a number of men and gave me valuable assistance in clearing the Communication Trenches.

(Sd) D.E.Crosbie, Capt. R.A.M.C.
M.O. i/c 11th.(S)Bn.Rl.Innis.Fus.

6.7.16.

SPECIAL ORDER OF THE DAY,
by
LIEUT-GENERAL Sir, T.L.N. MORLAND" K.C.B., D.S.O.,
3rd. July, 1916.

On the withdrawal of the 36th. Ulster Division into reserve after the desparate fighting of the last few days, the G.O.C. Xth. Corps wishes to express to the G.O.C. and all ranks his admiration of the dash and gallantry with which the attack was carried out which attained a large measure of success under unfavourable conditions.
He regrets the heavy and inevitable losses sustained and feels sure that, after a period of rest, the Division will be ready to respond to any call made upon it.

(Sd) G.Welsh, Br.Genrl.
D.A.&.Q.M.G., X Corps.

S P E C I A L O R D E R O F T H E D A Y.

BY MAJOR-GENERAL, O.S.W. NUGENT, D.S.O.

COMMANDING 36th. (ULSTER) DIVISION.

The General Officer Commanding the Ulster Division desires that the Division should know that, in his opinion, nothing finer has been done in the War than the attack by the Ulster Division on the 1st. July.

The leading of the Company Officers, the discipline and courage sgewn by all Ranks of the Division will stand out in the future history of the war as an example of what good troops, well led, are capable of accomplishing.

None but troops of the best quality could face the fire that was brought to bear upon them and the losses suffered during the advance.

Nothing could have been finer than the steadiness and discipline shown by every Battalion, not only in forming up outside its own trenches but in advancing under severe enfilading fire.

The advance across the open to the German line was carried out with the steadiness of a parade movement, under a fire both from front and flanks which could only have been faced by troops of the highest quality.

The fact that the objects of the attack on one side were not obtained is no reflection on the Battalions which were entrusted with the task.

They did all that man could do and in common with every Battalion in the Division shewed most conspicuous courage and devotion.

On the other side, the Division carried out every portion of its allotted task in spite of the heaviest losses.

It captured nearly 600 prisoners and carried its advance triumphantly to the limits of the objective laid down.

There is nothing in the operations carried out by the Ulster Division on the 1st. July that will nto be a source of pride to all Ulstermen.

The Division has been highly tried and has emerged from the ordeal with unstained honour, having fulfilled in every particular, the great expectations formed of it.

Tales of individual and collective heroism on the part of the Officers and Men com in from every side, too numerous to mention, but all showing that the standard of gallantry and devotion attained is one that may be equalled, but is never likely to be surpassed.

The General Officer Commanding deeply regrets the heavy losses of Officers and Men. He is proud beyond description, as every Officer and Man in the Division may well be, of the magnificent example of sublime courage and discipline which the Ulster Division has given to the Army.

Ulster has every reason to be proud of the men she has given to the service of our country.

Though many of our best men have gone the spirit which animated them remains in the Division and will never die.

(Sd) L. I. Comyn, Lieut. Col.
A. A. & Q. M. G.
36th. Division.

3rd. July, 1916.

109th. (ULSTER) BRIGADE.

ORDER OF THE DAY.

by

BRIGADIER GENERAL R. G. SHUTTER, D. S. O.

3rd. July. 1916.

The Brigadier General Commanding wishes to express his warm congratulations and high appreciation to all ranks of theBrigade on their gallant bearing and conduct during the great attack on the 1st. July.

The advance of the Brigade was so dashing, so resolute and determined that it was entirely irresistable and carried all before it, chasing the enemy in all directions and taking approximately 400 prisoners.

Each Battalion of the Brigade as was anticipated by all those who knew the grit and sterling qualities of the men of the Ulster Division vied with each other in deeds of personal gallantry and bravery, and the Brigade carried out to the letter the task which was entrusted to it of taking the "C" Line. In so doing the Brigade covered itself with undying fame and glory and its dashing determined advance and behaviour will undoubtedly undoubtedly go down to history as its share of the work of the great Ulster Division of Irish men

Unfortunately we have sustained grevious casualties but the Brigadier General hopes that when the ranks are presently filled with drafts, that wherever these may come from, the survivors of the original Brigade will do their utmost to instil their/own magnificient fighting spirit into the new arrivals, as by doing this they will be offering the most fitting tribute to their gallant dead comrades and friends who have fallen in honour on the Field of Battle, and who have left behind them such a splendid fighting record for those who come after them to live up to and emulate.

(Sd) A. C. Richardson.

Captain.
Brigade Major.
109th. Brigade.

CITY HALL,

BELFAST, 20th July, 1916.

SIR,

I have the honour to transmit herewith the enclosed Copy of Resolutions, which were unanimously passed by the Belfast City Council at their Meeting on the 19th inst.

I have the honour to remain, Sir,

Your obedient Servant,

(Sgd.) R. MEYER, Town Clerk.

-2-

Moved by THE LORD MAYOR,

Seconded by ALDERMAN DORAN, and unanimously

Resolved - "That we, the Lord Mayor, Aldermen, and Citizens of Belfast, acting by the Council, do hereby esteem it our honour and privilege to convey to the Officers, Non-Commissioned Officers and Men of the Ulster Division of his Majesty's Army our high admiration of their magnificent conduct in the successful attack on the German Lines in France, which began on Saturday, 1st July, when they were put to the supreme test, with the result known to the world - Viz., that they covered themselves with glory, the Officers leading their men with a gallantry to which justice cannot be done, and the men vieing with their Officers in deeds of heroism. The citizens reverently pay homage to the heroic dead - young men in the prime of manhood "who have laid down their lives and resigned the bright hopes of youth, and love, and ambition, to save their country from the fate of Belgium, Serbia, and Poland". To those who have been bereaved by the loss of their dear ones this Council tenders its most respectful and deepest sympathy, and prays that God will wipe away their tears and give them consolation. To the wounded the Council send their congratulations on their escape from death, and hopes for their speedy and complete recovery. To the Ulster Division and all sons of Ulster in his Majesty's armies this Council sends greeting and encouragement to uphold and strengthen the reputation they have already made on the battlefields of France and Flanders.

Moved by Councillor WHITE,

Seconded by Councillor WORKMAN, and unanimously

Resolved - "That those of us at home, keeping before us as an example the self-sacrifice of our gallant soldiers and sailors, should do all in our power by increased devotion and sacrifice on our part to carry the War to a successful issue, and so bring it to pass that our noble dead should not have died in vain".

P.T.O

-3-

    9th Royal Innis. Fus.
   10th Royal Innis. Fus.
   11th Royal Innis. Fus.
   14th Royal Irish Rifles.
  109th Machine Gun Coy.
  109th Light Trench Mortar Batty.

        For information and transmission to all concerned.

Ken. M. Moore
Captain,
Staff Captain,
109th Infy. Brigade.

31st July, 1916.

WAR DIARY

of

11TH (S) BATTALION ROYAL INNISKILLING FUSILIERS

FOR MONTH OF AUGUST, 1916

WAR DIARY

11th (S) Bn. Rl Inniskilling Fusiliers Army Form C. 2118.

Place	Date	Hour	Summary of Events and Information	Remarks and references to Appendices
Map Reference,	France	Sheet 28 S.W and 36 NW		
PLEOGSTEERT WOOD	1-8-16		In Trenches. Situation normal.	
	2-8-16		Situation normal. Casualties Capt. F C Mowbray. Artillery fine.	
	3-8-16		Situation normal. Battalion was relieved in the trenches by 9th Bn Rl Inniskilling Fusiliers	
ROMARIN			Battalion Headquarters and 'A','B' and 'C' Companies went back to ROMARIN to rest Billets. 'D' Company remained in Reserve at HILL 63. While out of Trenches Battalion is in Divisional Reserve.	
	4-8-16		Battalion Resting. 60 Other Ranks from 'A','B' and 'C' Companies proceeded to HILL 63 to be attached to 'D' Coy.	
	5-8-16		'D' Company working parties. Remainder training specialists. Draft of 8 Other Ranks from Base.	
	6-8-16		Battalion Bathing. 'D' Company Working parties. Remainder training specialists.	
	7-8-16		'D' Company working parties. Remainder training specialists. Working parties draft 1 Officer (2nd Lieut JJ Kennedy) 90 Other Ranks joined from notts and Derby Regiment. Lieut Col G H Borrah proceeded on leave, command of Battalion devolves on Captain W P Moore	
	8-8-16			

WAR DIARY 11th (S) Bn Rl Inniskilling Fus

INTELLIGENCE SUMMARY

Army Form C. 2118.

Place	Date	Hour	Summary of Events and Information	Remarks and references to Appendices
ROMARIN PLOEGSTEERT WOOD	9-8-16		Battalion Relieved 9th Bn Rl Inniskilling Fusiliers in trenches. Composite Company under Capt. J. E. Knott DSO, in Front Line Trenches. Composite Company under Lieut B.S. McCorkell in Subsidiary Line. Battalion Headquarters and Details under Capt J McCorkle at HILL 63. Relief completed at 11.45 p.m.	
	10-8-16		Situation normal. Casualties 14680 2/Lt J Doherty wounded Artillery Fire.	
	11-8-16		Situation normal.	
	12-8-16		Situation normal. Casualties 2nd Lieut A J F Ball wounded Artillery Fire. Draft 6 O.R. from 1st Battn.	
	13-8-16		Situation normal.	
	14-8-16		Situation normal. Casualties 17390 H/Cpl McKay, A wounded Artillery Fire Draft 22 other Ranks from Base.	
	15-8-16		Battalion was relieved in the trenches by 9 R Dub Fus. "B" Company remained in Reserve at HILL 63. "C" Coy	
ROMARIN			and A & D Coy went back to ROMARIN. "B" Company attached to "B" Company for working parties. Battalion in Divisional Reserve	
	16-8-16		Battalion Resting.	
	17-8-16		"B" and "C" Companies working parties. "A" & "D" Coys Specialists Training.	
	18-8-16		"B" and "C" Companies working parties. "A" & "D" Companies specialists training.	
	19-8-16		"B" and "C" Companies working parties. "A" & "D" Companies specialists training.	

WAR DIARY 11th (S) Bn. Rl. Innis. Killing Fusiliers

Army Form C. 2118.

INTELLIGENCE SUMMARY

(Erase heading not required.)

Instructions regarding War Diaries and Intelligence Summaries are contained in F.S. Regs., Part II. and the Staff Manual respectively. Title pages will be prepared in manuscript.

Place	Date	Hour	Summary of Events and Information	Remarks and references to Appendices
ROMARIN	20-8-16		'B' and 'C' Companies working parties. 'A' and 'D' Companies. Divine Service and Training. Major A.C. Pratt 9th R. Irish Fusiliers joined and took over Command of Battalion from Captain W. Moore. Notification received that Lieut H. Gallagher was awarded D.S.O, and 19929 Sergt J.A. Hunter the D.C.M. for gallantry on 1st July.	
	21-8-16		Commanding Officers inspection of all Companies. Battalion relieved the 9th Bn. Rl. Innis.Killing Fusiliers in the trenches. A + D Companies in the front line. B Company in the Subsidiary line	
PLOEGSTEERT WOOD			Battalion Headquarters and 'C' Company at HILL 63. Relief completed at 11.45 p.m. Casualties 32786 Pte J.C.Thomson, wounded rifle fire.	
	22.8.16		Situation normal.	
	23.8.16		Situation normal.	
	24.8.16		Situation normal.	
	25.8.16		Situation normal.	
	26.8.16		Situation normal.	
	27.8.16		Situation normal. 'C' Company Divine Service. Battalion to remain an extra day in the trenches. Draft of 9 Other Ranks from Base.	
	28.8.16		Situation normal. Battalion was relieved in the trenches by the 9th Bn Rl Innis Frs. Battalion	
ROMARIN			Headquarters and 'B' and 'C' Company went back to rest billets in ROMARIN. A Company remained in Reserve at HILL 63. D Coy attached to A Coy for working parties. Battalion in Divisional Reserve.	

WAR DIARY

11(S) Bn. Rl Inniskilling Fusiliers Army Form C. 2118.

INTELLIGENCE SUMMARY

(Erase heading not required.)

Place	Date	Hour	Summary of Events and Information	Remarks and references to Appendices
ROMARIN	29.8.16		Battalion Resting.	
	30.8.16		Battalion Bathing. 'A' & 'D' Coys Working Parties. B & C Companies Training.	
	31.8.16		'A' & 'D' Coys working parties. B & C Companies Training. Strength of Battalion 38 Officers and 605 Other Ranks.	

A.C. Pratt Major
Comm'd 11th Bn R Innis Fus

1.9.16

CONFIDENTIAL.

Original

S.9
109/36

WAR DIARY

of the

11th (SERVICE) BATTALION ROYAL INNISKILLING FUSILIERS.

From 1st September, 1916.   To 30th September, 1916

(VOLUME XII)

Vol 12

WAR DIARY of the 11th (S) Bn. Rl. Inniskilling Fusiliers

September, 1916

INTELLIGENCE SUMMARY

Army Form C. 2118.

Place	Date	Hour	Summary of Events and Information	Remarks and references to Appendices
			Map Reference Sheet 28 SW Belgium and France Scale 1/20.000 and Hazebrouck, Sheet 5A Scale 1/100.000	
ROMARIN	1-9-16		'A' and 'D' Coys working parties. 'B' + 'C' Coys training	
	2-9-16		'A' and 'D' Coys working parties. 'B' + 'C' Coys training	
	3-9-16		Divine Service. Battalion relieved the 9th Rl. Inniskilling Fusrs in the trenches. 'B' + 'C' Companies in the Front line, 'D' Company in the Subsidiary line and 'A'	
PLOEGSTEERT WOOD			Company and Battalion Headquarters at Hill 63. Relief completed at 10.35 p.m. Brigade order received that the Battalion remain in line for three days and then move to new sector.	
	4-9-16		Situation normal.	
	5-9-16		Situation normal.	
	6-9-16		Situation normal. Battalion was relieved in the trenches by the 10th Worcester Regiment (57th Bde) Battalion Headquarters and 'A' and 'D' Companies went back to Rest Billets in ROMARIN. 'C' Company remained in Reserve at STIRLING CASTLE,	
ROMARIN			HILL 63. 'B' Coy attached to 'C' Coy. Battalion in Divisional Reserve. Lieut. K. A. Murphy & 2nd Lieut. T. C. Sweeney joined for duty.	

59

September, 1916. WAR DIARY of the 11th (S) Bn, Rl. Inniskilling Fusiliers

or

INTELLIGENCE SUMMARY

Army Form C. 2118.

II

Place	Date	Hour	Summary of Events and Information	Remarks and references to Appendices
ROMARIN	7-9-16		Battalion moved to new Brigade area at DRANOUTRE. Route T27.d - T26.d - KORTEPYP - CABT - BREEMEERSCHEN - ZWARTEMOLENKOEK - DRANOUTRE to N.32 Central. Battalion Headquarters and 'A' and 'D' Companies left ROMARIN at 1 p.m. 'B' and 'C' Companies left STIRLING CASTLE about the same time. The Battalion arrived at N.32 Central at 5.30 p.m. Battalion in Brigade Reserve. Lieut A.H.Muir & Lieut J.Scott joined the Battalion for duty. Cpl Wilson B Artillery Coy. 23649 notification received that 17212 A/Cpl R. Maybly is awarded military medal	Appendices Nos. 3 map
DRANOUTRE	8-9-16		Ordinary training & working parties	
	9-9-16		Ordinary training & working parties	
	10-9-16		Divine Service & working parties	
	11-9-16		Ordinary training & working parties. Men of HQrs and Derby Regiment attached, are now transferred & given Inniskilling number.	
	12-9-16		Battalion relieved the 9th Rl Inniskilling Fusiliers in the Brigade trenches taking over the left 'Ball' Sector as per attached map. 'A' Company are on the Right of the line, their trenches include the BULL RING (about 45 yards from the German lines) 'D' Coy on the left of the line, 'C' Coy in support, and 'B' Coy in reserve.	

WAR DIARY of the 11th (S) Bn. Rl. Inniskilling Fusiliers

September, 1916 — Army Form C. 2118.

Place	Date	Hour	Summary of Events and Information	Remarks and references to Appendices
DRANOUTRE	12-9-16		The Battalion on the Right in the 14th Rl. Irish Rifles and on the Left the 4th Canadian Division. Relief commenced 4.30 p.m & completed at 7.10 p.m. Situation normal.	
	13-9-16		Situation normal.	
	14-9-16		Situation normal. Artillery fired into our support lines. Casualties 14892 Cook Sgt. T. Miller, 20877 L/Cpl W Johnston, 23401 Pte S/smith HJ, 11297 Pte J G Ichurst, 14897 Pte E. Murphy, 19927 Pte J Hempsey, wounded artillery fire, all these men were cooks. Notification received that 15241 C.S.M. S. Bulloch has been awarded the Military Cross & 14117 Cpl. J. Reilly the Distinguished Conduct Medal for gallantry on the 1st July 1916. 2nd Lieut R.H. Tallot joins for duty.	
	15.9.16		During the day, Situation normal. In the evening the Battalion carried out a raid on the German trenches opposite the Bull Ring. At 8.47 a party of 44 N.C.O's & men under 2nd Lieut. T. Adams left our lines & a few minutes later were in the German lines. They remained in the German trenches for about 10 minutes & returned. The Raiders had splendid co-operation from the artillery. The Barrage was practically impassable. The main object of the raid, to obtain prisoners or other means of identification, to kill Germans, & to find out of enemy are manning &	

September, 1916. WAR DIARY of the 11th (S) Bn. Royal Inniskilling Fusiliers. Army Form C. 2118.

INTELLIGENCE SUMMARY.

Place	Date	Hour	Summary of Events and Information	Remarks and references to Appendices
DRANOUTRE	15.9.16		Nature of enemy trenches. The result was one prisoner & very heavy German casualties. Our casualties were 18279 L/Cpl Wray C, 17390 L/Cpl M'Kay A, 14736 Pte Taylor R, 23413 Pte Gibson A all missing. 43018 Pte Pich J.S, 14703 Pte McConnell J, 17250 L/Cpl S. and J.R.B all wounded. (Appendix C'O's report) The 10th Bn carried out a raid on our right at the same time.	Appendix No 2. Report
	16.9.16		During the day our Artillery bombarded the German lines & hostile wire doing great damage. Casualties 19242 Sgt Wing D.S, 40048 Pte Banks J.W, 18674 Pte Rutledge J, all wounded by premature fixed mortar bomb. Canadian artillery. During the night the Canadian Division on our left carried out a raid on the enemy lines. Our sector was quiet.	
	17.9.16		Situation normal. Casualties 43023 Pte J. Scattergood killed rifle fire.	
	18.9.16		Battalion was relieved in the trenches by the 9th R. Inniskilling Fusiliers and took over billets at WAKEFIELD HUTS, DRANOUTRE	
	19.9.16		Battalion Resting	
	20.9.16		Training & Bathing. Notification received that 19929 Sergt J.A Hunter awarded medal of St George 3rd Class.	

WAR DIARY of 11th (S) Bn. Rl Inniskilling Fusiliers

September, 1916

INTELLIGENCE SUMMARY
V

Army Form C.2118.

Place	Date	Hour	Summary of Events and Information	Remarks and references to Appendices
DRANOUTRE	21-9-16		Training & Bathing. Blu	
	22-9-16		Training, Bathing. Forenoon training, Afternoon Battalion paraded at 12.30 p.m. and marched to BAILLEUL and were entertained to a Cinema entertainment + his 9 afterwards were allowed 2 hours to visit the town. Battalion fell in at 7.30 p.m + marched back to billets. Blu	
	23-9-16		Draft of 2nd Lieuts S. Patterson + 67 Other Ranks Battalion Training. Blu	
	24-9-16		Quine Somme. Battalion relieved the 9th Rl Inniskilling Fusiliers in the trenches. B & C Coy in the front line, 'A' Coy in support, 'D' Coy in Reserve to the 16th Irish Division are on our left. Situation normal. Blu	
	25-9-16		Situation normal. Blu	
	26-9-16		Situation normal. Blu	
	27-9-16		Situation normal. Blu	
	28-9-16		Brigade Trench howitzer Battery took action enemy lines from 9 a.m. to 10.30 a.m. Notification received that 14919 Sgt J. O'Hara, 4036 L/Cpl H. Ferns and 14703 Pte J. McConnell are awarded the Military Medal for gallantry on night of 15th Sept during raid on enemy trenches. Blu	

September 1916 WAR DIARY of the 11th (S) Bn. R. Inniskilling Fusiliers

Army Form C. 2118.

INTELLIGENCE SUMMARY

Place	Date	Hour	Summary of Events and Information	Remarks and references to Appendices
DRANOUTRE	29.9.16		Situation normal. Casualties Capt H C Gordon 28577 Pte E McCauley + 17905 Pte J Grindle all wounded Artillery fire. Wh.	
	30.9.16		Situation normal. Wh. Battalion was relieved in the Trenches by the 9th Bn. R. Inniskilling Fusiliers and went back to Rest Billets at Aircraft Farm, N32 Central Wh.	
			Strength of Battalion 41 Officers 633 Other Ranks Wh.	

A.C. Pratt Lieut Col,
Comdg, 11th (S) Bn. R. Inniskilling Fusiliers

S E C R E T.
Reference Map.
28 S.W. 1/20,000.

War Diary
Appendix No 2.

Report on raid on enemy trenches carried out by 11th (S) Bn.
Royal Inniskilling Fusiliers on night 15th/16th September, 1916.

1. Intention.	The raid was carried out with the object of:- (a) taking prisoners and procuring identification, capturing or destroying machine guns and emplacements. (b) to kill Germans. (c) to obtain information regarding enemy trenches, to ascertain if gas was installed and finally any evidence of mining.
2. Point of exit from our trenches.	N.30.c.37.15 (South corner of BULL RING.)
3. Point of entry enemy trenches.	N.30.c.52.15 (45 yards east of point of exit from our trenches).
4. Number of party.	1 Officer (2nd Lieut. T.Adams) and 44 other ranks, divided into 5 blocking parties, 1 prisoners party and 1 examining party.
5. Weapons.	Bayonet men - rifles and bayonets and 6 bombs each. Throwers - Revolvers or knobkerries and 10 bombs each. Carriers - Rifle and bayonet and 18 bombs each. Prisoners party and examining party - same as throwers. In all about 360 bombs and 5 P bombs and 4 nosebags ammonal, in addition were taken 2 scaling ladders, 1 bangalore torpedo(which was not used), 14 wire cutters, 4 grapnels and ropes(not used) 24 electric torches, 1 dinner bell(for signal purposes) and 1 tape.
6. Method of Conducting.	Party crossed over our parapet at 8.45 p.m. Moon rising but still behind a cloud. Formed up unobserved in large shell crater 25 yards outside our parapet. Rushed remaining 20 yards to enemy parapet through what was practically a gap in enemy wire. Enemy sentry on left challanged the raiding party as leaders were mounting the parapet and fired two rounds without effect. But before whole raiding party gained enemy trench stray bullets from enemy machine gun cross fire in NO MAN'S LAND accounted for two of our casualties.

No.1.Party proceeded South down the enemy front line trench where enemy was met in considerable numbers. Our party opened on them with bayonets and then bombs. The enemy beat a hasty retreat down the trench but were held up by our Artillery Box Barrage which had been opened and they were forced back on to our party who engaged them strongly and accounted for at least eight German casualties, most of whom it is thought are killed. One prisoner was taken by this party. In addition a dug-out was bombed but the result is not known. The dug-out was deep and the sound of the bombs exploding was very muffled. There was only one entrance to the dug-out and it went under their front line parapet. Sets of equipment were seen on the fire step and these were thrown out over the parapet but they could not be collected.
The casualties to our No.1.Party were as follows:-

L/Cpl. Wray.	"the leader"	missing
Pte. McConnel		wounded
" Taylor.		missing
" Doherty.		wounded.
" Gibson.		Missing.

P.T.O.

L/Cpl. Wray having used all his bombs collected some German No.1 Grenades and used them with great effect. Particularly good work was done by L/Cpl. Wray, Pte. McConnell and Pte. Dodwell.

No.2. Party.

This party got over the enemy parapet and found themselves about 5 yards to the left (North) of the communication trench down which they were to go with the object of blocking it. They inadverdently passed the entrance to the trench (it did not look like an entrance as it had been blown so wide by previous shell fire) but after proceeding some 20 yards the leader Sergt O'Hara recognised the fact that this place must have been the entrance. He and party returned, bombing their way back as the enemy were bombing them from 2nd line. The party led by L/Cpl. Fern then bombed their way to the 2nd line. They came to a large dug-out on the right at the junction of communication trench and 2nd line which Pte ORGILL bombed apparently with great sucess as loud screams and shouts were heard. There was also a small dug-out opposite the large one out of which Germans came. The enemy by now were collecting in strength but as they clustered together our party did great execution by very accurate bombing and revolver shooting and thus caused at a low estimate 10 - 20 casualties and throughly flustered the enemy, unfortunately all the bombs were used up but they continued with rifles and revolvers until the signal to retire came.
They were unable to make any headway as the enemy kept getting further reinforcements.
Casualties to this party were as follows:-
    L/Cpl. McKay, A.   Missing.

No.3. Party.

This party had been ordered to go up the front line trench to the North and block it. On entering the trench and turning to the left a party of about half a dozen Germans were seen, these they proceeded to bomb and they retired hurriedly, L/Cpl. Donaldson caught up one and got to grips with him, the L/Cpl. had a Mills bomb in his hand with pin in, with this weapon he hit the German finishing him off with his Knobkerrie. Cpl. Donaldson only sustained the loss of one trouser leg which the German tore from him. The party then proceeded up the trench to the place they had to block.
No dug-outs, no M.G. emplacements and no gas cylinders were seen.
Casualties to this party were as follows:-
    Pte. Graydon   wounded (slightly)
    Pte. Bradbury   wounded (slight)
    L/Cpl. Large.   wounded (slight).

No.4. Party.

This party had been ordered to go down the 2nd line trench to the South. This party followed No.2 Party (which could not get to their objective) The No.4 Party therefore could not get through to their objective, so they backed up No.2 Party and bombed the 2nd line trench.
Casualties to this party were as follows:-
    Pte. Suttle   wounded (slight)

No.5. Party.

This party finding the communication trench blocked with No.2 and No.4 Parties went along the front line to left and right and assisted No.1 and No.3 Parties.
Casualties to No.5 Party were as follows:-
    L/Cpl. Sea.   wounded (slight)
    Pte. Peck.   wounded (bullet)

Enemy Wire: In poor condition, thin, chiefly knife rests, gaps in places.

Trenches. Front line 7ft.6in. deep, corduroyed, revetted with hurdle work, 2ft wide at bottom, 3ft at top, strutted across top of

9. DUG-OUTS. Not much information on this point. One large dug-out at junction of communication trench and 2nd line appears to be deep and have two entrances.

10. Estimated casualties.
    (a) Our own:
    Killed. Nil.
    Missing. 4
    Wounded 9
    (b) Enemy:
    At least 33 in addition to any casualties in the large dug-out.

11. Prisoners. One prisoner was brought in, papers and documents were forwarded to 9th Corps.

12. Summary. The enemy trenches successfully entered.
    Identification obtained.
    Enemy appeared to be distinctly "flustered".
    Our party returned in good spirits.
    No sign of gas cylinders, mining operations seen.
    Information obtained regarding nature of enemy trenches.
    Enemy casualties treble our own.
    Capable leadership by 2nd Lieut. T. Adams.
    Capable leading of parties by Sergt. O'Hara, L/Cpl. Wray, and L/Cpl. Donaldson.
    Good work by L/Cpl. Fern and Pte's Bodwell and Utgill.

(Sgd) A.C. Pratt, Major,
Comdg. 11th Bn. R.-Innis. Fus.

16/9/16.

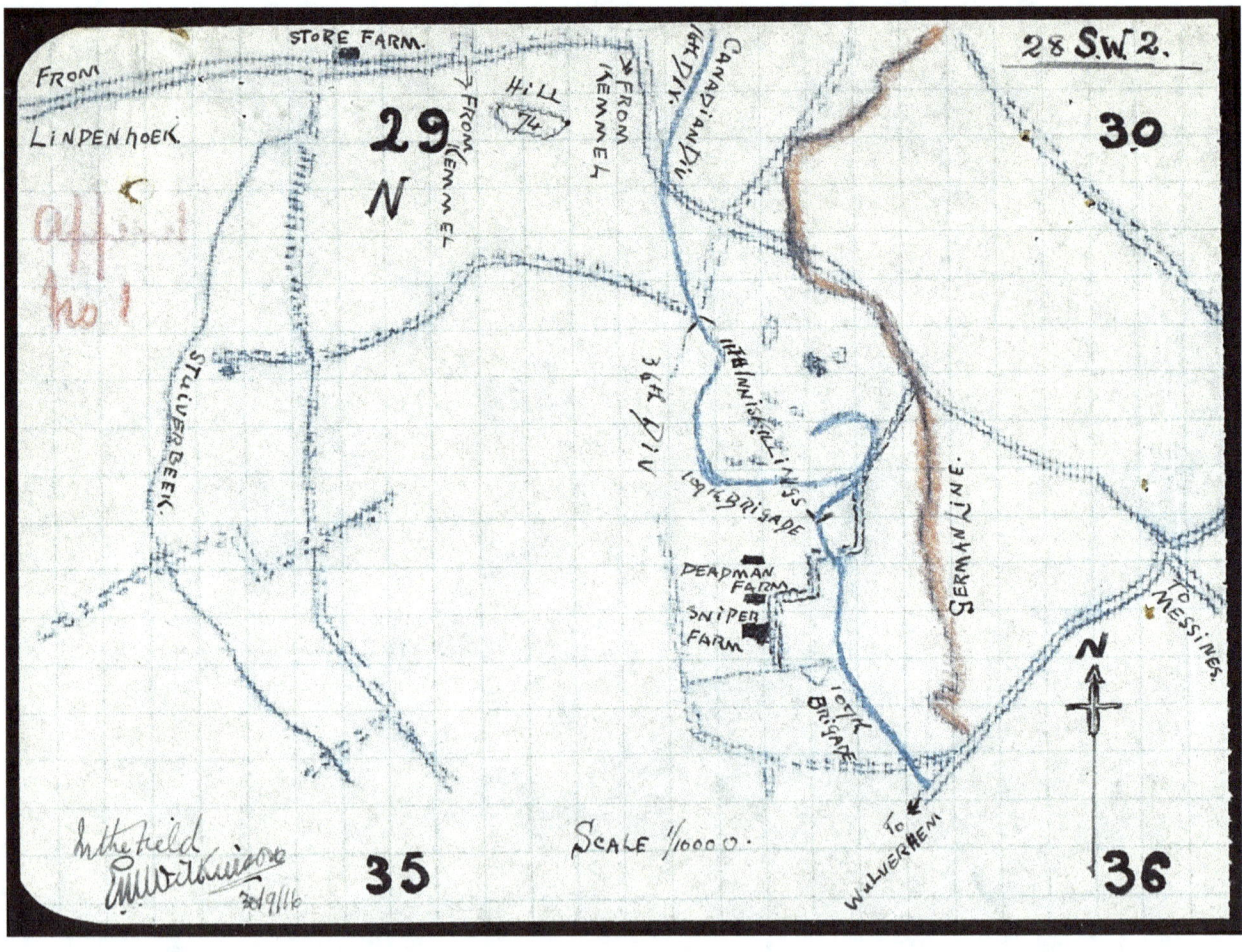

ORIGINAL.

Confidential

VOL 13

S.10

WAR DIARY

of

11th (SERVICE) BATTALION ROYAL INNISKILLING FUSILIERS

From 1st OCTOBER, 1916   To 31st OCTOBER, 1916.

(VOLUMN XIII.)

Army Form C. 2118.

WAR DIARY of 11th (S) B. R.I. Inniskilling Fusiliers

October, 1916

INTELLIGENCE SUMMARY

(Erase heading not required.)

Place	Date	Hour	Summary of Events and Information	Remarks and references to Appendices
			Map Reference HAZEBROUCK 5A and BELGIUM and FRANCE Sheet 28.S.W 1/20,000	
AIRCRAFT FARM N.32 Central.	1.10.16		Working Parties & Bathing. Enis.	
	2.10.16		Working Parties Enis.	
	3.10.16		Working Parties Enis.	
	4.10.16		Working Parties. Notification received that 2nd Lieut T Adams is awarded the MILITARY CROSS for gallantry during raid on 15th/16th Sept. & 14735 Pte A.Taylor & 18279 P/Cpl C. Wray are awarded the MILITARY MEDAL for gallantry on the 1st July 1916. Enis	
	5.10.16		Working Parties Enis	
	6.10.16		Battalion relieved the 9th R. Inniskilling Fusiliers in the trenches 'A' and 'D' Companies in the front line, 'B' Coy in support & 'C' Company in reserve Lieut. Col F.E. Pratt proceeded on leave, Major J.E. Knott DSO assumes command	
SPANBROEK SECTOR	7.10.16		Situation normal Enis.	
	8.10.16		Situation normal Enis.	

WAR DIARY of 1st (S) Bn. Royal Innishilling Fusiliers

October 1916

INTELLIGENCE SUMMARY

Place	Date	Hour	Summary of Events and Information	Remarks and references to Appendices
SPANBROEK SECTOR	9-10-16		Situation normal. 28954 Pte Hampson A, 14494 Pte Collins A, 17248 Pte Cullen J. and 19192 Pte McHenry D all wounded artillery fire. Acting return received that 13134 Reg't. Sergt. Major J. Bleakly is awarded MILITARY CROSS for gallantry on 1st July 1916.	
	10-10-16	At 2 a.m. G.S. was discharged from our sector & artillery bombarded enemy's lines. An officer's patrol went out after gas was discharged but was unable to reach enemy's lines. We had no casualties. Remainder of day Situation normal.	
	11-10-16		Situation normal. Casualties 15249 Pte Lilleck J, 14040 Pte Cluff C, 43007 Pte Searles J, 17959 Pte Proctor J and 20602 Pte Weadin H all wounded, rifle grenade fire.	
	12-10-16	At 2.30 pm the 9th Bn. R.I. Innis Fus'rs made a successful raid on the German lines from our sector, capturing two prisoners. Our casualties were 43014 Pte Clarke J.T. and 43015 Pte Fenwick G. Killed and 43013 Pte Doney R. wounded, all by Rifle grenade fire.	
WAKEFIELD HUTS, DRANOUTRE	13.10.16		Battalion was relieved in the trenches by the 9th R.I. Innis Fus'rs & went back to Divisional Reserve at WAKEFIELD HUTS, DRANOUTRE. Companies at disposal of Company Commanders. Afternoon Company Officers inspection of Companies.	

October 1916 WAR DIARY of 11th (S) Bn. RI Inniskilling Fusiliers Army Form C. 2118.

or

INTELLIGENCE SUMMARY

(Erase heading not required.)

Place	Date	Hour	Summary of Events and Information	Remarks and references to Appendices
WAKEFIELD HUTS DRANOUTRE	14.10.16		Forenoon Bathing. Afternoon Football. Notification received that Sergt. W. Hand is awarded MILITARY MEDAL for services in the field.	
	15.10.16		Forenoon Divine Service. Afternoon - Football "C" "D" Coys in final of inter-company match. "D" Coy 3 goals "C" Coy 1 goal.	
	16.10.16		Training.	
	17.10.16		Forenoon Ordinary training. Afternoon Battalion marched to BAILLEUL & visited to Cinema. Those afterwards who were interested to do & allowed to visit the town. Battalion fell in at 7 p.m. & marched back to rest camp.	
	18.10.16		Battalion relieved the 9th R. Innis Frs in the trenches, B & C Coy in the front line A Coy in support & D Coy in reserve. Relief completed at 5.30 p.m. Hdqt. at O.B.Pratt rejoined from leave & resumed Command.	
SPANBROEK SECTOR	19.10.16		Situation normal.	
	20.10.16		Situation normal.	
	21.10.16		Situation normal.	
	22.10.16		Situation normal.	
	23.10.16		Situation normal.	
	24.10.16		Situation normal. The Battalion was relieved in the trenches by the 9th R. Innis Frs	

October 1916. WAR DIARY 11th (S) Bn. Rl. Inniskilling Fusiliers Army Form C. 2118.
or
INTELLIGENCE SUMMARY.

(Erase heading not required.)

Instructions regarding War Diaries and Intelligence Summaries are contained in F. S. Regs., Part II. and the Staff Manual respectively. Title pages will be prepared in manuscript.

Place	Date	Hour	Summary of Events and Information	Remarks and references to Appendices
DERRY CAMP N32 Central	24.10.16		Withdrew to Brigade Reserve at DERRY CAMP N32 Central. Situation normal.	
	25.10.16		Working Parties. Situation normal.	
	26.10.16		Working Parties. Situation normal.	
	27.10.16		Working Parties power.	
	28.10.16		Working Parties. Situation normal.	
	29.10.16		Divine Service & Working Parties, chiefly of 2 & Other Ranks, gunners from the Base Ships.	
SPANBROEK SECTOR	30.10.16		Battalion relieved the 9th Bn. Rl. Inniskilling Fusiliers in the trenches. A & D Coys in front line. 'C' in support & 'B' Coy in Reserve. Situation normal.	
	31.10.16		Strength of Battalion 39 Officers 677 Other Ranks. Situation normal.	

A. C. Pratt Lieut-Col.
Comdg. 11th (S) Bn. Rl. Inniskilling Fusiliers

CONFIDENTIAL

WAR DIARY

of

11th ROYAL INNISKILLING FUSILIERS,

From 1st November 1916 to 30th November 1916.

WAR DIARY
11th (S) Bn. Rl Inniskilling Fusiliers

November, 1916

Army Form C. 2118.

Instructions regarding War Diaries and Intelligence Summaries are contained in F.S. Regs., Part II. and the Staff Manual respectively. Title pages will be prepared in manuscript.

INTELLIGENCE SUMMARY
(Erase heading not required.)

Place	Date	Hour	Summary of Events and Information	Remarks and references to Appendices
			Map reference HAZEBROUCK SW 5ª and 28 SW 1/20,000	
SPANBROEK Sector	1.11.16		In the Trenches. Situation normal. Casualties 18690 Pte T Wightman Rifle Grenade Fire 29068 Pte C Walsh Wounded Trench Mortar Fire	
	2.11.16		Situation normal. Casualties 22956 Pte G Taylor wounded by rifle grenade fire	
	3.11.16		Situation normal. Casualties 22587 L/Cpl J J Walker Killed by Rifle fire	
	4.11.16		At 3.15 p.m. our Trench Mortar Batteries & Artillery bombarded the enemy's line. Enemy's retaliation our casualties were 1 killed 5 wounded	
	5.11.16		Battalion was relieved in the Trenches by the 9th Bn Rl Inniskilling Fusiliers and went back to WAKEFIELD HUTS, DRANOUTRE. Battalion in Divisional Reserve	
DRANOUTRE	6.11.16		"G" Company (Raiding Party) commenced training. Remainder Training & working parties	(1) Scheme for Raid (2) Programme of training for week
	7.11.16		"G" Company training and bathing. Remainder working parties	
	8.11.16		"G" Company training. Remainder Bathing & Working Parties & Training	
	9.11.16		"G" Company training. Remainder Training, Practice "Alarm" Battalion ready to move off complete in 34 minutes	

1577 Wt. W.10791/1773 500,000 1/15 D.D.&L. A.D.S.S./Forms/C. 2118.

Army Form C. 2118.

WAR DIARY
or
INTELLIGENCE SUMMARY.

November 1916   11th (S) Bn Rl Inniskilling Fusiliers

(Erase heading not required.)

Instructions regarding War Diaries and Intelligence Summaries are contained in F. S. Regs., Part II. and the Staff Manual respectively. Title pages will be prepared in manuscript.

Place	Date	Hour	Summary of Events and Information	Remarks and references to Appendices
DRANOUTRE	10.11.16		"D" Company Training. Remainder Route March and Musketry	
SPANBROEK Sector	11.11.16		Battalion relieved the 9th Bn Rl Inniskilling Fusiliers in the trenches. "B" and "C" Coys in the front line. "A" Coy in Support and "D" Coy in Reserve. "G" Company remained at WAKEFIELD HUTS. Situation normal. 14154 Serjt A Galbraith & 13472 Pte Tagg S F both wounded by rifle fire.	
	12.11.16		Situation normal	
	13.11.16		Situation normal	
	14.11.16		Situation normal	
	15.11.16		A bombardment with Trench Mortars & Artillery on enemy lines opposite our sector during the day. Situation normal.	
	16.11.16		At 10 p.m. we raided the German lines with 4 Officers & 184 Other Ranks ("G" Coy). The raiding party remained in the German lines for 1 hour, captured 3 prisoners & inflicted considerable casualties and damage on the enemy. Our casualties were 2 killed & 14 Wounded. Situation normal. The Battalion was relieved in the trenches by the 9th Bn Rl Inniskilling Fusiliers and went back to DERRY CAMP (N 32 Central) Bull Show in Brigade Reserve	(1) C.O. Report (2) Copy of Congratulations
DERRY CAMP N32 Central	17.11.16			

WAR DIARY

November 1916 11th (S) Bn. R. Innskilling Fusiliers

INTELLIGENCE SUMMARY

Army Form C. 2118.

Place	Date	Hour	Summary of Events and Information	Remarks and references to Appendices
DERRY CAMP	18.11.16		Nothing particular	
	19.11.16		Nothing particular. Divine Service	
	20.11.16		Nothing particular. Casualties 43009 Pte Draper W. 26085 Pte D. and W. Killed and 43001 Pte Day W.A. Wounded all by Trench Mortar Fire	
	21.11.16		Nothing particular	
	22.11.16		Nothing particular	
	23.11.16		Ordinary training & C.O's Inspection	
SPANBROEK Sector	24.11.16		The Battalion relieved the 9th R. Innskilling Fusiliers in the trenches. 'A' and 'D' Coy in the front line, 'B' Coy in support & 'C' Coy in Reserve. During the day, Situation normal. Casualties 43050 Pte Nally. T Wounded. At 10 p.m the enemy started a violent bombardment on our front and support lines, this was posted over an hour. Our casualties were 9 killed & 12 Wounded	
	25.11.16		Situation normal	
	26.11.16		Situation normal	

WAR DIARY

November 1916   11th (S) Bn. Rl Inniskilling Fusiliers

INTELLIGENCE SUMMARY

Place	Date	Hour	Summary of Events and Information	Remarks and references to Appendices
SPANBROEK Sector	27.11.16		Situation Normal. A Patrol under 2nd Lieut STRONG visited the German lines & left a letter, written by one of the prisoners captured by us on night 16/17th November also a notice saying that if any of the enemy wanted to surrender they would be well treated.	
	28.11.16		Situation Normal.	
	29.11.16		Situation Normal. Battalion was relieved in the trenches by the 9th Rl Innis Fusiliers & went back to Divisional Reserve at WAKEFIELD Huts, DRANOUTRE.	
DRANOUTRE	30.11.16		Battalion Resting. Strength of Battalion 30.11.16 41 Officers 625 Other Ranks	

A.C. Pratt.
Lieut. Col.

Comdg. 11th (S) Bn Rl Inniskilling Fusiliers

SECRET.   Copy No 8a Appendix No 1

SCHEME TO RAID ENEMY TRENCHES, LEFT SUB-SECTOR, 109th BRIGADE.

Reference :- 1. Attached Map taken from Aeroplane Map
I.B. 712, B? N.30.a.o.d. dated 21.10.16

2. Trench Map 36 S.W.3. 1/10,000.

1. OBJECT.

A. To raid enemy trenches between N.36.a.31.94 and N.30.c.37.48.
B. To kill Germans.
C. To gain indentification.
D. To capture or destroy Machine Guns.
E. To discover if there is gas installed.
F. To examine tunnell sloping towards our line at N.30.c.43.40, vide report on Raid by 9th R. Inniskilling Fus: 11/12th October.

2. TROOPS ENGAGED.

4 Officers and 174 Other Ranks, with the addition of :-

(a) 2 R.E. (Tunnelling Company)
(b) 4 R.E. (150th Field Coy. R.E.)

Total. 4 Officers and 180 Other Ranks.

3. DISTRIBUTION.

In four parties as follows :-

RIGHT PARTY.   Off. N.C.O. Men.
No.1 Squad.   Ammonal tube party.   -   1   3
    2   "   (Right 1st Line Blocking
               Party.   -   1   4
             (Search Party.   -   -   2
    3   "   (Back Communication trench
               Blocking Party.
             a.(Trolley line.   -   1   5
               (Search Party.   -   -   2
             b Right Back Communication
               Trench Blocking Party.   -   1   5
             c.(Right 3rd line Blocking
               Party.   -   1   5
               (Search Party.   -   -   2
               (Lewis Gun Party.   -   1   3
    4   "   (Right 2nd Line Blocking
               Party.   -   1   5
             (Search Party (Dugout V)   -   -   2
    5   "   Centre 2nd line Blocking
               Party.   -   1   4
    6   "   Pivot Party.   1   1   4
                                            TOTAL.   1   9   46

RIGHT CENTRE PARTY.

			Off.	N.C.O.	Men.
No.1 Squad.	Ammonal tube party.		-	1	3
2 "	Right 1st Line Blocking Party.		-	1	4
3 "	{ Back Communication Trench Party.		-	1	3
	{ Search Party.		-	-	3
4 "	{ Right 2nd Line Blocking Party.		-	1	4
	{ Search Party. (Dugout 5)		-	-	2
5 "	Centre 2nd Line Blocking Party.		-	1	4
6 "	Pivot Party.		1	1	3
		TOTAL.	1	6	33

LEFT CENTRE PARTY.

			Off.	N.C.O.	Men.
No.1 Squad.	Ammonal tube party.		-	1	3
2 "	Right 1st Line Blocking Party.		-	1	4
3 "	{ Right 2nd Line Blocking Party.		-	1	4
	{ Search Party (Dugout 7)		-	1	3
4 "	{ Forward Tramway Blocking Party.		-	1	5
	{ Search Party.		-	-	2
5 "	{ Left Fork Communication Trench Blocking Party (Back Blocking Party)		-	1	5
	{ Search Party.		-	-	3
	{ Lewis Gun Party.		-	1	3
6 "	Pivot Party.		1	1	3
		TOTAL.	1	7	35

LEFT PARTY.

			Off.	N.C.O.	Men.
No.1 Squad.	Ammonal tube Party.		-	1	3
2 "	{ Left 1st Line Blocking Party.		-	1	7
	{ Search Party.		-	-	2
3 "	{ Right 1st Line Blocking Party.		-	1	5
	{ Search Party.		-	-	2
4 "	{ Communication Trench Blocking Party.		-	1	7
	{ Search Party.		-	-	2
5 "	Pivot Party. Search Party.		1	1	3
		TOTAL.	1	5	30

4. ### ARMS AND EQUIPMENT.

BAYONET MEN.

Rifles and bayonets - 50 Rounds Ammunition -
4 Bombs

One Bayonet man of each squad to carry a torch and a pair of wire cutters on rifle.

Two bayonet men per party (total 8 in all) will have their rifles fitted with cups for firing Mills grenades.

THROWERS.
11 bombs each carried in haversack and 4 in pocket.
One knobkerrie or a revolver if expert with them and twenty rounds of ammunition.

CARRIERS.
15 bombs carried in a bucket and 10 in haversack.
One knobkerrie.
Carriers of flanking parties going to positions where the wind is suitable will each have two M.S.K bombs (to be carried with detonator seperate)

SEARCHERS.
Fifty per cent, 15 bombs in a sandbag also one M.S.K. Bomb (with detonator seperate) carried in pocket, the other fifty per cent to carry two ammonal bags or pea bombs.
The whole in addition carrying either an axe hammer or a knobkerrie or a revolver, also an electric torch and three Mills bombs in pockets.

AMMONAL TUBE PARTY (1 N.C.O. & 3 men).
Carry an ammonal tube with detonator and primer and spare detonator and two primers.
In addition each man to carry in his pockets 4 bombs, and either a knobkerrie or revolver with 20 rounds of ammunition.
Each squad leader to carry a pair of wire nippers, an electric torch with red paper over bulb, 4 bombs in pockets and either a knobkerrie or revolver with 20 rounds of ammunition.

LEWIS GUN PARTY.
Two men with gun and spare parts bag, remainder 6 magazines each in sandbags.
The whole, revolvers and 20 rounds of ammunition.
1 torch for party.

R.E.
Arms and equipment as ordered by O.C. Unit.

OFFICERS.
One Very pistol - four green lights and four red lights. One revolver and 20 rounds of ammunition. One wire cutter. One torch.

OFFICER'S ORDERLY.
Same as bayonet men.

ALL.
No marks of identification will be carried. Faces & hands will be blacked with burnt cork.
White armlets will be worn on each arm, these will have a khaki cover to be pulled off the arm on entry to trench.
Steel helmets will be worn. P.H.Gas Helmets to be carried in flap of coat.

MOVEMENT ACROSS NO MAN'S LAND.

Parties leave our lines as follows.

No. 1. Party.   N.30.c.35.18.   } BULL RING.
    2.   "   N.30.c.40.22.   }
    3.   "   N.30.c.35.28.   - WORCESTER ALLEY.
    4.   "   N.30.c.15.34.   CLOGHER VALLEY.

POINT OF ENTRY.

The parties will enter the enemy trenches at same time at points:-

    No. 1 Party.   @ N.30.c.54.05 Point marked 2
     2   "   @ N.30.c.54.15   "   "   3.
     3   "   @ N.30.c.50.29   "   "   4.
     4   "   @ N.30.c.43.40   "   "   5.

ACTION ON ENTERING ENEMY TRENCHES.

No. 1 Party. On entering trench blocking party will proceed along trench (South), leaving pivot party at entrance and block at Point X.2. Remainder proceed East up Communication trench to enemy 3rd line blocking at point marked X.3,a,b & c, leaving 2 blocking parties at points X.4 and X.5.

No. 2 Party. On entering trench blocking party proceed along trench (South), leaving pivot party at entrance and block at point Y.2. Remainder proceed up to enemy 3rd line trench to point Y.3. leaving parties at Y.4 to deal with Dugout marked U and block trench at point Y.4 and Y.5.

No. 3 Party. On entering trench blocking party will proceed to the right (South) some 10 yards and block at point B.2. Two parties proceeding East up trench to tramway to B.3 and 4 and block there. The remainder proceed N.E. to point B.5, and block, leaving a pivot party at point of entry. The party proceeding to B.3 dealing with dugout marked T

No. 4 Party. On entering trench blocking party will proceed to the Left (North) and block at point A.2, also a party to the Right (South) and block at point A.3. Remainder to proceed North to enemy 2nd line and block at point A.4., leaving party at entrance of line to deal with tunnell previously mentioned.

SIGNALS.

(1) Signals for Artillery barrage will be called for by telephone from the BULL RING, point N.30.x.40.45, failing this 1 green rocket from this point for 1st phase, one green rocket and golden chain rocket for 2nd phase.

Officers i/c raiding parties will carry Very pistols and coloured lights so that in the event of a barrage not being called for just when they require it, they will be able to call on the O.C. Battalion by a signal of one green rocket fired towards the BULL RING.

(2) Signal for withdrawal.
Two red parachute lights fired in the direction of the enemy lines from the BULL RING.

AMMONAL TUBE PARTIES.

These parties will lay their tube in the wire ready to fire at Zero time.
After entry into enemy trenches, Ammonal tube party with Right Party will join No. 2 Squad.
Of Right Centre Party to No. 4 Squad.
Of Left Centre Party to No. 3 Squad
Of Left Party to No. 8 Squad.

1 Man, 15th R.E., will accompany each party and is included in the numbers in the distribution.

Two Men, Tunnelling Company will accompany and are included in the distribution of No. 5 Squad left party.

ARTILLERY AND TRENCH MORTAR BARRAGE.

10.   There will be no previous artillery barrage, but for several days prior to the raid our T.M.s will as far as possible thin and damage the enemy wire. Bangalore Tubes and wire cutters will be used to do the rest. A Box Barrage by artillery and T.M.s will be arranged with the O.C. Group Artillery, to be put on when called for by a pre-arranged signal.

Machine guns and Lewis guns will fire outside our flanks.

SEARCH PARTIES.

11.   Searchers, who will each have an electric torch, will be given their various objectives, they will be attached to blocking parties and work in rear of them. They will be also used as carriers until entry into enemy trenches, they will dump their burdens at the points of entry leaving them to be looked after by the pivot parties.

2nd PHASE OF ACTION.

12.   On completion of clearance of enemy's 1st, 2nd and 3rd lines the 2nd Phase will begin.

A raid will be made on the enemy's 4th line by the Right and Left Centre Parties making as their objectives the points indicated L & N respectively.

Right Party.   Squads 3 a & b and Squad 5 Objective L
Left/Party   Squads 2, 3 & 4 Objective N.
 Centre
Left Party, No.3 Squad proceeds to point marked P.
            No.2 Squad proceeds to point marked O.
            No.4 Squad proceeds to point marked Q.

The 2nd Phase will not begin until a signal of two green rockets has been fired from our lines.

WITHDRAWAL FROM.

13.   The parties will withdraw on prearranged signal.
The back communication trench blockers will retire on their respective pivots, then the centre trench parties. The last to retire will be the front line blockers.

The men in the various squads should be told off in little parties of 2 & 3 and each should have a good idea of where his comrade is.

POINTS OF SPECIAL NOTE.

14.   The length of the line to be raided is about 280 yards. The depth of line taken in enemy 1st, 2nd and 3rd lines.

The knowledge gained from the raid of the 9th Royal Inniskilling Fus on night of 11/12th October that a tunnel exists at point of entry of No 4 party has decided the most Northerly objective. The centre and right are undoubtedly the most sporting part of the proposed raid as they contain tramway and trolley line and large dugouts, the point where No 2 party is to enter is the point where we successfully raided on night 15/16 th September, though at that time the enemy wire was weaker and the concertina wire on top of trench was non-existent.

Page 6.

An advantage that will be gained from positions of our Trench and enemy trench is that the enemy will have difficulty in putting down a barrage to stop our withdrawal similarly the proximity will enable us to get up reserves of ammunition and grenades.

An important point which it is difficult to illiminate is the danger of one party bombing another.

In order to obviate this danger as far as possible, One electric torch with thin red paper over the bulb will be carried by each squad. If a squad suspects that it is being bombed by another party of our squads, the red light on a rifle will be held up in the trench.

Small modifications may have be made in view of new Aeroplane photographs and other information which may come to hand.

The part of NO MAN'S LAND to be traversed has been reconnoitred by us frequently but no further to the Right (South) though 300 - 500 yards to the Left (North).

15.   MISCELLANEOUS.

Dummy screens will be used on the flanks to draw the enemy fire.

The bombers will be fully instructed in the use of the German hand grenades. Similarly the Lewis Gunners in the use of the German Machine Gun.

16.   DATE AND PROPOSED TIME OF RAID.

Entry into enemy trenches at the rise of the Moon 7.45 p.m. on Tuesday 14th November.

Zero time therefore 7.45 p.m.

                                           A. C. Pratt.
                                                Lieut-Co
                    Comdg. 11th (S) Bn. Rl. Inniskilling Fusiliers.
8.11.16.

Copy. No. 1.   109th Brigade
  "   " . 2.   O. C. 11th Inniskillings
  "   - 3.   Major Knott. D.S.O
  "   " . 4.   O. C. "A" Company.
  "   " . 5.   O. C. "B"   "
  "   " . 6.   O. C. "C"   "
  "   " . 7.   O. C. "D"   "
  "   " . 8.   War diary
  "   " . 8a   "   "
  "   " . 9.   Office.

11th (S) Bn. Rl. Inniskilling Fusiliers.

Appendix No 2

"G" COMPANY.

Scale of Training Parades.

Monday Nov. 6th.	9.0 a.m.	Parties to be told off into their respective squads and leaders selected.
	10.0 a.m.	March out by Parties to ground and explanation of scheme, first to Officers, then to N.C.O.s and men by O.C. parties.
	2.0 p.m.	Bayonet Fighting.
	2.30 p.m.	Physical Training.
	3.0 p.m. to 4.30 p.m.	Lewis Gunners - Ammonal tube party - Bombers with MSK, P and Rifle Bombs - Lecture to searchers. Remainder:- Bombing and revolver shooting for those carrying revolvers.
Tuesday Nov. 7th.	9.0 a.m.	Physical Training.
	9.30 a.m.	Bayonet Fighting.
	10.15 a.m. to 12.30 p.m.	Right and Left Centre Parties on ground in dummy trenches.
	10.15 a.m. to 11.30 a.m.	Right Centre and Left Parties - Specialists. Remainder Bombing and revolver shooting.
	11.30 a.m. to 12.30 p.m.	Right Centre and Left Parties - Use of German Grenades.
	2.0 p.m. to 4.30 p.m.	Right Centre and Left Parties on ground in dummy trenches.
	2.0 p.m. to 3.30 p.m.	Right and Left Centre Parties - Specialists. Remainder Bombing, Revolver shooting.
	3.30 p.m. to 4.30 p.m.	Right and Left Centre Parties - Use of German Grenades.
Wednesday Nov. 8th.	9.0 a.m.	Physical Training.
	9.30 a.m.	Bayonet Fighting.
	10.15 a.m. to 12.30 p.m.	Right Centre and Left Parties on ground in trenches and parctise withdrawal.
	10.15 a.m. to 11.30 a.m.	Right and Left Centre Parties - Specialists Remainder bombing.
	11.30 a.m. to 12.30 a.m.	Right and Left Centre Parties - Use of German Grenades.

P. T. O.

Wednesday Nov.8th	2.0 p.m. to 4.30 p.m.	Right and Left Centre Parties on ground and in trenches - Practice withdrawal.
	2.0 p.m. to 3.20 p.m.	Right Centre and Left Parties - Specialists. Remainder, bombing.
	3.30 p.m. to 4.30 p.m.	Right Centre and Left Parties - Use of German Grenades - Questioning - Explanation of German Dugouts.
Thursday Nov.9th.	9.0 a.m.	Physical Training.
	9.30 a.m.	Bayonet Fighting.
	10.15 a.m. to 12.30 p.m.	All Specialists. Remainder - Bombing, any not having used bombs to throw live bombs.
	2.0 p.m. to 3.0 p.m.	Lecture to Right and Right Centre Parties on procedure in trenches. Duty of all to obtain identification. Responsibility to bring back casualties. Economy of bomb supply. Action on stink bombs being thrown. Explanation of signals
	6.0 p.m. to 8.0 p.m.	Right and Right Centre Parties - Night rehersal on ground. Left and Left Centre Partues - Night rehersal on ground. Dummy bombs to be carried and thrown. Advance as from our lines. Practise withdrawal. Should be done twice.
Friday Nov.10 th	9.15 a.m.	Physical Training.
	10.15 a.m.	Full dress rehersal by day. Dummies to be carried and thrown. Practice dealing with prisoners and supply of bombs.
	2.0 p.m. to 2.30 p.m.	Bayonet Fighting.
	2.30 p.m. to 3.0 p.m.	Point out any mistakes that occurred during the morning
	3.0 p.m. to 4.30 p.m.	Specialists) with a view to correcting by Remainder bombing) practice mistakes that occurred during the morning Special instruction of all in throwing from strutted A framed trenches.
		Patrols from 2 Coys.

P.

Saturday Nov. 11th.	9.0 a.m.	Physical Training.
	9.30 a.m.	Bayonet Fighting.
	10.15 a.m. to 12.30 p.m.	Specialists Remainder bombing and practising throwing bombs from strutted trenches.
	2.0 p.m. to 3.0 p.m.	Interior economy, fitting bands, issue of torches etc.
	6.0 p.m. to 8.0 p.m.	Fulldress night rehersal. All parties.
Sunday, Nov. 12th.		Church Parade.
	2.0 p.m. to 4.0 p.m.	Full dress day rehersal.
Monday Nov. 13th.	9.0 a.m.	Physical Training.
	9.30 a.m.	Bayonet Fighting
	10.0 a.m. to 12.30 a.m.	Inspection of outfits.

SECRET.
Ref. Map 28 S.W.
1/20,000

Appendix
No 3

REPORT ON RAID ON ENEMY'S TRENCHES CARRIED
OUT BY 11th (S) BATTALION ROYAL INNISKILLING FUS.
ON NIGHT 16/17TH NOVEMBER, 1916.

(1) Intention. The raid was carried out with the object of

   (a) Raiding the enemy trenches between N.36.a.31.94 and N.30.c.37.48
   (b) To Kill Germans
   (c) To gain identification.
   (d) To capture or destroy Machine Guns.
   (e) To discover if there is gas installed.
   (f) To examine tunnel sloping towards our line at N.30.c.43.40 (Vide report on raid by 9th R. Innis. Fus. 11/12th October, 1916)

(2) Troops Employed

4 Officers (2nd Lieuts. STRONG, JOHNSTONE, MALSEED, TALBOT) and 184 Other Ranks, including 1 N.C.O. 171st Tunnelling Coy. R.E.

(3) Point of Exit.

No.1 Party (D Coy.)   N.30.c.36.18
No.2   "   (C Coy.)   N.30.c.40.22
No.3   "   (B Coy.)   N.30.c.35.22
No.4   "   (A Coy.)   N.30.c.13.34

(4) Zero Time.

10 p.m. Moon ¼ full, rose 9.58 p.m.

(5) Time of leaving our trenches.

No.1 Party (minus) – 35 Minutes.
No.2   "   "   – 25   "
No.3   "   "   – 25   "
No.4   "   "   – 45   "

(6) Point of entry into enemy trenches.

No.1 Party – N.30.c.54.06
No.2   "   – N.30.c.54.18
No.3   "   – N.30.c.59.28
No.4   "   – N.30.c.43.40

(7) Weapons.

<u>Ammonal Tube Party.</u> Each man 4 Mills No. 5 Grenades Knockberrie. Leader 1 revolver, 1 wire cutter, 1 torch.
<u>Bayonet men.</u> Rifles, Bayonets, each 14 Mills No. 5 Grenades, 30 rounds S.A.A. 50% torch on rifles.
<u>Throwers.</u> Revolver or Knockberrie and 29 Mills No. 5 Grenades.
<u>Carriers.</u> Rifle and bayonet, 20 Mills No. 5 Grenades (selected carriers 1 M.S.K. Bomb.)
<u>Searchers.</u> 50% Rifle & Bayonet.
        50% Knockberrie or revolver and 25 No. 5 Mills Grenades.
        50% carried a torch.
<u>Lewis Gun Party.</u> Lewis Gun, 12 Magazines and each man 4 Mills No. 5 Grenades, 1 revolver (three of above parties)
<u>Officers.</u> 1 Torch, 1 pair wire cutters, 1 revolver, 1 Very Pistol with Red and Green Lights, and 4 Mills No.5 Grenades.

(8) Signals.

For artillery, Trench Mortar, and M.G. Box Barrage by telephone and by 1 Green and 1 red rocket.
For "running short of Bombs" (for raiding party leaders to O.C. Battalion) 1 Green Very Light fired towards our parapet.
For withdrawal 2 red parachute rockets.

2/

(9)
Method of Conducting.

All 4 parties left our parapet to time, headed by their ammonal tube parties crawled to selected position mostly shell craters close to enemy parapet.

No. 1 Party "D" Company.

Ammonal tube exploded at Zero.
Party rushed over enemy parapet, a German near entrance dashed at our leading man but was at once killed.
Party as detailed proceeded East up Main communication trench and the other parties as detailed along front line. Party proceeding to right (S) along enemy front line met a party of enemy bombers who retired before our party, leaving 4 killed, this party then blocked trench at their objective. The party which proceeded N of C.T. reached 2nd Line, the C.T. beyond this point was blocked with concertina wire evidently just pulled in there. Enemy sniper behind it fired on our men wounding one, he was then bombed and fired no more. This party blocked trench at the point where the wire was pulled down.
The Right Second Line Party proceeding South met with opposition but reached their objective passing large dugout which was empty and which they blew up. This party counted 10 dead enemy, and in addition making use of their own bombs and bombs supplied by No.3 Party they had a spirited contest with an enemy counter-attacking party.
They altogether expended 42 sacks of bombs, or in other words 630 Bombs apparently with a great deal of success, and the estimate of casualties to the enemy they put at the moderate figure of 20 to 30.
There is no Gas installed in 1st or 2nd Line.
1st Line Trench - sides boarded, "A" Frames strutted at top - 2½' wide at bottom.
3½' at top, 6' deep - much damaged by shell fire. Duckboarded.
A machine Gun emplacement in 1st Line at N.30.c.53.01 This gun was firing, the position was beyond the outside objective but was reached by our bombers who put it out of action but could not reach it owing to the trench being very strongly wired.

No. 2 Party "C" Company

Ammonal tube party were discovered while placing tube and were bombed. They suffered two casualties, and most unfortunately the tube was also bombed and exploded. The Officer i/c of the party finding the party on his right has effected an entrance led his men there.
From here they worked to their objectives with the exception of some 6 men who joined on to No.1 Party.
They worked up their own C.T. as far as the 2nd line gaining the important objective of a large dugout where they accounted for 7 Germans and the dugout with a bag of ammonal. On their way to this point they accounted for one German in the front line and also demolished what appeared to be a snipers post.
No signs of gas being installed in these trenches.
2nd Line is a broad trench with trollyway 2'6" gauge. 6' deep, 4" wide at bottom 10' wide at top. In bad condition much knocked about by shell fire.
The main C.T. is also in a very bad condition, sides being knocked in by T.M. Bombs and is deep in mud.
The front line trench is a better and a safer one than the 2nd line.
No signs of Trench Mortar or M.G. emplacements or mining.
This party sent in one wounded prisoner of 104th Saxon Regiment.

No.3 Party "B" Company.	They exploded their ammonal tube at Zero. Parties rushed in just as previously rehearsed. Right front line party met with opposition and were bombed successfully by the enemy but pushing on reached their objective and accounted for 4 Germans.

The left front line party also met with strong opposition and suffered casualties, but being reinforced they pushed back the enemy who left two dead.

The Right 2nd Line party reached their objective, a large dugout which they bombed killing two of the enemy as they ran away. They partially demolished this dugout, blowing the back out of it, it was one of the metre thick concrete dugouts. The forward party with Lewis Gun reached their objective without casualties but with plenty of fighting. The Lewis Gun team fired eleven magazines upon a party of the enemy who were organising a counter-attack from their 3rd Line. This counter-attack completely collapsed under this Lewis Gun fire. The Lewis Gun was invaluable.

This party captured 2 prisoners., one of whom was found at the bottom of a shaft which was either a listening gallery or a mine shaft - N.30.c.52.23. This prisoner was a miner and was sent under special escort to the Brigade to be cross examined he appeared willing to give away plenty of information.

The shaft whatever it was, was full of water and was blown in with ammonal bags.

No signs of gas being installed.

1st/in moderate/in bad condition. 2nd Line trench in
Line Trench   bad condition

There is no wire between 1st and second line. Duckboards are not continuous in front line and non-existant in 2nd Line. Signs of trolley in 2nd Line but broken up by our shells and b-

4th Party. "A" Company.	Ammonal Tube party had much difficulty with their tube and were discovered and bombed by the enemy, but the party cont. their efforts until both the tube and the party were put out of action by enemy bombs.

Being unable to gain an entrance the Officer i/c of the party sent back a report to the O.C. Battalion who ordered their retirement.

(10) BARRAGE	The barrage of the Artillery, the Trench Mortars and Machine guns could hardly have been better. The barrage was put on the moment it was asked for and well maintained.
(11) ENEMY FIRE.	The reply of enemy artillery was negligible though their Trench Mortars were active and obtained direct hits on N.29.a. trench and on PICCADILLY.
(12) OUR CASUALTIES.	Officers Nil. Other Ranks. Killed 1 Missing 1 Wounded 14 Total: 16

The body of the man killed was brought in.

(13) REMARKS.	The difficulty and necessity for careful organisation in supply of Mills No. 5 Grenades.

The necessity of every man previous to raid having training in NO MAN'S LAND, also in being taught to use the German hand grenade.

The use of the Lewis Gun to prevent or break up a counter-attack.

(14).
RESULTS:

(a) Enemy 1st and 2nd Line trenches raided from N.30.c.48.32 to N.30.c.54.01.

(b) Casualties to enemy at a low estimate 60 Killed and wounded, exclusive of those accounted for by the barrage.

(c) Identification obtained - 3 prisoners captured.

(d) Information that no gas is installed.

(e) Maps, Documents, Gas Helmets and sundry articles of equipment brought back.

(f) Increased morale to our troops.

(Sgd) A.C. Pratt, Lt. Col.
Commanding 11th-(S) Bn. R. In. Fus.

In the Field,
    17th Nov. 1916.

Extract from :-

BATTALION ROUTINE ORDERS
by
LIEUT-COL. A.C. PRATT
COMMANDING, 11th(S)Bn. R.INNIS. FUSLRS.
18.11.16.

1105. **SPECIAL ORDERS.**

The following is an extract from Divisional Routine Order No. 1258 dated 17th November, 1916.

"The Divisional Commander congratulates the 11th Royal Inniskilling Fusiliers on their successful raids carried out last night.

Most valuable information has been gained from the prisoners taken at a moment when information of suspected German reliefs was urgently required.

The series of raids were admirably planned and carried out in most gallant style. The conduct and high spirit of the raiding parties are worthy of special commendation and are charactistic of the spirit of the Division".

The following telegrams have already been received :-
(i) From the Army Commander to convey his congratulations to those concerned in the success of the raid and to state that very valuable information was obtained thereby in addition to the damage inflicted on the enemy.

(ii) From the Brigadier to O.C. 11th R. Innis. Fus. "Heartiest congratulations to you and your splendid Battalion."

(iii) From 49th Brigade:- "G.O.C. and all ranks heartily congratulate Col. Pratt and 11th Inniskillings on their successful enterprise."

(iv) From 47th Brigade:- "Heartiest congratulations on your success from Irish friends in 47th Brigade."

(v) Several other Commanders and Units and all three Battalions in the Brigade have offered us very sincere congratulations.

The Commanding Officer wishes also to take this opportunity of congratulating all ranks on the splendid work done. The raiders have brought much honour on themselves and on the Regiment.

CONFIDENTIAL

WAR DIARY

of

11TH BATTALION ROYAL INNISKILLING FUSILIERS

from

1st December 1916

to

31st December 1916

CONFIDENTIAL.

ORIGINAL.

WAR DIARY

of the

11th (SERVICE) BATTALION ROYAL INNISKILLING FUSILIERS.

FROM 1st DECEMBER, 1916.   TO 31st DECEMBER, 1916.

(VOLUME XV.)

CONFIDENTIAL.

WAR DIARY or INTELLIGENCE SUMMARY

Army Form C. 2118.

of 11th (S) Bn. Rl. Innis Killing Fuslrs.

December, 1916

Place	Date	Hour	Summary of Events and Information	Remarks and references to Appendices
			Map Reference, HAZEBROUCK SHEET 5A and SHEET 28 S.W. 1/20,000	
WAKEFIELD HUTS DRANOUTRE	1.12.16		In Divisional Reserve. Ordinary Training.	
	2.12.16		Training. Football Match 14th R. Irish Rifles 3 11th R. Innis Fus. 3 goals	
	3.12.16		Dump Service.	
	4.12.16		9th Battalion left WAKEFIELD HUTS, DRANOUTRE at 2.15 p.m. and marched via NEUVE EGLISE to BULFORD CAMP, KORTE PYP, arriving there for the night.	
KORTE PYP	5.12.16		9th Battalion left BULFORD CAMP at 10 a.m. and marched via RED LODGE to relieve the 6th South Lancashire Regiment in the trenches, taking over the DOUVE	
DOUVE SECTOR BOIS DE PLOEGSTEERT			Sector of the Bois de PLOEGSTEERT. Relief was completed at 12 noon. Situation normal.	
	6.12.16		Draft of 37 arrived from Base. Situation normal.	
	7.12.16		Situation normal. 2/Lt. J.J. McGhee killed rifle fire.	
	8.12.16		Situation normal.	
	9.12.16		Situation normal. Draft of 26 O.R. arrived from base.	
	10.12.16		Situation normal.	
	11.12.16		Situation normal.	
	12.12.16		Situation normal.	
	13.12.16		The Battalion was relieved in the trenches by the 10th Bn. R. Innis Killing Fuslrs & went back to the GALLERIES, HYDE PARK CORNER, relieving the 9th Bn. R. Innis Killing Fus.	
HYDE PARK CORNER BOIS DE PLOEGSTEERT	14.12.16		In Brigade Reserve.	
	15.12.16		Working Parties. Draft of 71 O.R. arrived from base. Working Parties.	

WAR DIARY

December 1916 of 11th (S) Bn. Rl Inniss Fusilliers

INTELLIGENCE SUMMARY

Army Form C. 2118.

Place	Date	Hour	Summary of Events and Information	Remarks and references to Appendices
HYDE PARK CORNER	16.12.16		Working Parties.	
BOIS DE PLOEGSTEERT	17.12.16		Working Parties.	
	18.12.16		Working Parties.	
	19.12.16		Working Parties.	
	20.12.16		Afternoon. The Battalion marched to KORTEPYP and were inspected by the Commander in Chief Genl. Sir Douglas Haig. Afternoon Working Parties.	
	21.12.16		The Battalion relieved the 10th Bn Rl Innis Killing Fusiliers in the trenches, 2 Coy each of B & C in the front line, Remaining ½ Coys in HALFWAY HOUSE, "A" Coy in Subsidiary line & "D" Coy in Reserve at HYDE PARK CORNER.	
DOUVE SECTOR	22.12.16		Situation normal.	
BOIS DE PLOEGSTEERT	23.12.16		Situation normal.	
	24.12.16		Situation normal. No 19662 C.Q.M.S. W.J. Beatty wounded with fire.	
	Xmas		Situation normal. Artillery active on both sides, at 8.30 p.m the 25th Division on our right carried out a raid, bombardment lasted 3/4 hr. Company as carried out inter company relief, ½ of A & D Coys in front line. Remaining ½ Coys in "HALF WAY HOUSE", B Coy in Subsidiary line & "C" Coy in Reserve at HYDE PARK CORNER.	
	26.12.16		Situation normal.	
	27.12.16		Situation normal. Draft of 15 O.R joined from base. Notification received that No 14673 2/Lt R Dunhill, 18634 Sgt D. Th. Blakley & 17360 Pte H McCarthy had been awarded the Military Medal for bravery in the field during big mining 1916.	
	28.12.16		Situation normal.	

Army Form C. 2118.

WAR DIARY
or
INTELLIGENCE SUMMARY

December 1916   of 11th (S) Bn. Rl. Inniskilling Fusrs.

(Erase heading not required.)

Place	Date	Hour	Summary of Events and Information	Remarks and references to Appendices
HYDE PARK CORNER BOIS DE PIECQUEBERT	29.12.16		Situation normal. The Battalion was relieved in the trenches by the 10th Bn Rl Innis Fusrs & went back to Brigade Reserve. 'A', 'B' and 'D' Coy. in GALLERIES, HYDE PARK CORNER and 'C' Coy at RED LODGE.	
	30.12.16		Working Parties, 2/Lieuts R H Rutledge and G Peake Gorland joined for duty.	
	31.12.16		Divine Service & Working Parties.	
			Strength of Battalion 41 Officers & 804 Other Ranks	

A. C. Pratt Lieut. Col.
Comdg. 11th (S) Bn. Rl Inniskilling Fusiliers

CONFIDENTIAL   ORIGINAL

WAR DIARY

of the

11th (SERVICE) BATTALION ROYAL INNISKILLING FUSILIERS.

From 1st JANUARY, 1917   To 31st JANUARY, 1917.

(VOLUME XVI.)

WAR DIARY or INTELLIGENCE SUMMARY

January 1917 — 11th (S) Bn. RI Inniskilling Fus. Army Form C. 2118.

Place	Date	Hour	Summary of Events and Information	Remarks and references to Appendices
GALLERIES HYDE PARK CORNER	1.1.17		Map Reference HAZEBROUCK 5A and Belgium and France Sheet 28 S.W. 1/20.000. Holiday. Christmas festivities held to-day, everyone had a good time. Lieut. Col. A.C. Pratt proceeded on leave. Command of Battalion devolves on Major J.E. Knott D.S.O.	Mine.
	2.1.17		Working Parties	Mine.
	3.1.17		Working Parties	Mine.
	4.1.17		Working Parties	Mine.
	5.1.17		Working Parties. Notification received that Lieut. Col. Pratt has been awarded the D.S.O. and Captain D.E. Crosbie R.A.M.C. and Captain J.S. Hyles the Military Cross	Mine.
	6.1.17		The Battalion relieved the 10th Bn. R.I. Inniskilling Fusiliers in the trenches taking over a greatly extended sector to the right and left of the MESSINES Road, B. and C. Coys. in the front line and A & D Companies on the Subsidiary line. Bn. H.Q. at LIMABADY LODGE HILL 63. Situation normal	Mine.
DOUVE SECTOR	7.1.17		Situation normal	Mine.
	8.1.17		Situation normal	Mine.
	9.1.17		Situation normal	Mine.
	10.1.17		Situation normal. Company is carried out inter-company relief A+D front line B+C Coys in support.	Mine.

WAR DIARY or INTELLIGENCE SUMMARY

January 1917 — 11th (S) Bn Rl Inniskilling Fusiliers

Army Form C. 2118.

(Erase heading not required.)

Place	Date	Hour	Summary of Events and Information	Remarks and references to Appendices
Douve Sector	11.1.17		Situation normal.	
	12.1.17		Situation normal.	
	13.1.17		Situation normal.	
	14.1.17		Situation normal. Battalion was relieved in the trenches by the 10th Rl. Inniskilling Fusiliers & went back to Brigade Reserve. A & D Coys at Red Lodge, B & C Coys	
Galleries Hyde Park Corner			& H.Q. at Galleries, Hyde Park Corner.	
	15.1.17		Situation normal. Working Parties.	
	16.1.17		Working Parties.	
	17.1.17		Working Parties.	
	18.1.17		Working Parties.	
	19.1.17		Working Parties.	
	20.1.17		Working Parties.	
	21.1.17		Working Parties.	
	22.1.17		The Battalion relieved the 10th Rl. Inniskilling Fusiliers in the Douve Sector. B & C Coys in front line & A & D Coys in support. Relief was greatly hindered by an enemy Bombardment & Raid. Relief commenced at 2 p.m. and completed about 9 p.m. Our Casualties were 3 O.R. wounded. Trench line shelled & flare & Trench Mortar in place.	

Army Form C. 2118.

WAR DIARY or INTELLIGENCE SUMMARY

January 1917   11th (S) Bn Rl Inniskilling Fusrs

(Erase heading not required.)

Instructions regarding War Diaries and Intelligence Summaries are contained in F.S. Regs., Part II. and the Staff Manual respectively. Title pages will be prepared in manuscript.

Place	Date	Hour	Summary of Events and Information	Remarks and references to Appendices
DOUVE SECTOR	23.1.17		Situation normal. MMG	
	24.1.17		Situation normal. MMG	
	25.1.17		Situation normal. MMG	
	26.1.17		Situation normal. Companies carried out inter-company relief. A & D Coys in front line & B & C Coys in Support. Hard frost continues MMG	
	27.1.17		Situation normal. MMG	
	28.1.17		Situation normal. MMG	
	29.1.17		Situation normal. MMG	
	30.1.17		The Battalion was relieved in the Trenches by the 10th Bn Rl Inniskilling Fusrs and went back to Brigade Reserve in GALLERIES HYDE PARK CORNER. Casualties 4 killed 2 wounded MMG. Working Parties. MMG	
GALLERIES HYDE PARK CORNER	31.1.17		Strength of Battalion 38 Officers 812 Other Ranks MMG.	

Comdg 11th (S) Bn Rl Inniskilling Fusiliers

Vol 17

S14

WAR DIARY

of

11th BATTALION ROYAL INNIS. FUSILIERS.

From 1st February 1917
To 28th February 1917.

WAR DIARY or INTELLIGENCE SUMMARY.

January 1917 11th (S) Bn. Rl. Inniskilling Fusrs Army Form C. 2118.

Place	Date	Hour	Summary of Events and Information	Remarks and references to Appendices
DOUVE SECTOR	23.1.17		Situation normal.	
	24.1.17		Situation normal.	
	25.1.17		Situation normal.	
	26.1.17		Situation normal. Companies carried out inter-company relief. A & D Coys in front line & B & C Coys in Support. Hard Frost continues	
	27.1.17		Situation normal.	
	28.1.17		Situation normal.	
	29.1.17		Situation normal.	
	30.1.17		The Battalion was relieved in the Trenches by the 10th Bn Rl Inniskilling Fusrs and was sent to Brigade Reserve at GALLERIES HYDE PARK CORNER Casualties 4 Killed 2 Wounded	
GALLERIES HYDE PARK CORNER	31.1.17		Working Parties. Strength of Battalion 38 Officers 812 Other Ranks.	

Comdg 11th (S) Bn Rl Inniskilling Fusiliers

Vol 17

S14

WAR DIARY

of

11th BATTALION ROYAL INNIS. FUSILIERS.

From 1st February 1917
To 28th February 1917.

ORIGINAL.

WAR   DIARY

of the

11th. (SERVICE) BATTALION ROYAL INNISKILLING FUSILIERS.

From 1st. FEBRUARY, 1917.   To 31st. FEBRUARY, 1917.

(VOLUME XV11.)

WAR DIARY or INTELLIGENCE SUMMARY

Army Form C. 2118.

of 11th (S) Batt. R. Inniskilling Fusiliers

February 1917

(Erase heading not required.)

Place	Date	Hour	Summary of Events and Information	Remarks and references to Appendices
GALLERIES			Map Reference HAZEBROUCK 5A and Belgium and France Sheet 28 S.E. 1/20,000, 28 S.W. 1/20,000	
HYDE PARK CORNER	1/2/17		Battalion in Brigade Reserve, working parties hard. Gen.I.	
	2/2/17		Working Parties. Gen.I.	
	3/2/17		Working Parties. Gen.I.	
	4/2/17		Working Parties. Gen.I.	
	5/2/17		Working Parties. Gen.I.	
	6/2/17		Working Parties. Gen.I.	
	7/2/17		The Battalion relieved the 10th R. Inniskilling Fusiliers in the DOUVE SUB SECTOR	
DOUVE SECTOR			"C" and "B" in the Front Line and "D" and "A" in support, stating Gens. continues. Gen.I.	
	8/2/17		Situation Normal. Gen.I.	
	9/2/17		Situation Normal. Gen.I.	
	10/2/17		Situation Normal. Gen.I.	
	11/2/17		Companies carried out inter company relief "C" and "D" in Front Line "B" and "A" in support. Stat. Gen.I.	
	12/2/17		Situation Normal. Gen.I.	
	13/2/17		Situation Normal. Gen.I.	

Army Form C. 2118.

WAR DIARY
or
INTELLIGENCE SUMMARY.

(Erase heading not required.)

of 11th & 13th Bat. R. Inniskilling Fusiliers

February 1917.

Instructions regarding War Diaries and Intelligence Summaries are contained in F. S. Regs., Part II. and the Staff Manual respectively. Title pages will be prepared in manuscript.

Place	Date	Hour	Summary of Events and Information	Remarks and references to Appendices
DOUVE SECTOR	14/2/17		Situation normal.	
	15/2/17		Battalion was relieved in the trenches by the 10th Bat R. Inniskilling Fus. and moved to Brigade Reserve at GALLERIES, HYDE PARK CORNER. Hard frost.	
GALLERIES HYDE PARK CORNER	16/2/17		Battalion resting and fitting out. Draft 20 O.R. joined from Base. Thaw severe.	
	17/2/17		Working Parties.	
	18/2/17		Working Parties.	
	19/2/17		Working Parties.	
	20/2/17		Working Parties. Raining.	
	21/2/17		Working Parties.	
	22/2/17		The Battalion relieved the 10th Bat R. Inniskilling Fusiliers in the DOUVE SUB SECTOR. B and C in the front line and A and D in supports.	
DOUVE SECTOR	23/2/17		Situation normal.	
	24/2/17		The Battalion was relieved in the trenches by the 5th Bat. R. Irish Rifles and took the Brigade Reserve at GALLERIES, HYDE PARK CORNER.	
GALLERIES HYDE PARK CORNER	25/2/17		The Battalion left HYDE PARK CORNER at 11 a.m. and marched via DESEULE BAILLEUL and METEREN to PRADELLES arriving in Billets at 5 p.m. Dinner was served on road. Battalion now in Divisional Reserve for training.	
	26/2/17			

T1134. Wt. W708—776. 500000. 4/15. Sir J. C. & S.

Army Form C. 2118.

WAR DIARY

or ~~INTELLIGENCE SUMMARY~~ of 11th SD Batt. R. Inniskilling Fr.

(Erase heading not required.)

Instructions regarding War Diaries and Intelligence ___ February 1917
Summaries are contained in F. S. Regs., Part II.
and the Staff Manual respectively. Title pages
will be prepared in manuscript.

Place	Date	Hour	Summary of Events and Information	Remarks and references to Appendices
PRINCESS M.	27/2/17		Battalion resting and fitting out.	
	28/2/17		Training.	
			Strength of Battalion 34 Officers 819 Other Ranks.	

Wint. Major.
Comdg. 11th SD Batt. R. Inniskilling Fusiliers.

CONFIDENTIAL.

W A R   D I A R Y

of

11th BATTALION ROYAL INNIS. FUSILIERS,

from 1st March 1917.

to 31st March 1917.

Army Form C. 2118.

WAR DIARY
INTELLIGENCE SUMMARY

March 1917 of the 11th (S) Bn. R. Inniskilling Fusiliers.

(Erase heading not required.)

Instructions regarding War Diaries and Intelligence Summaries are contained in F.S. Regs., Part II. and the Staff Manual respectively. Title pages will be prepared in manuscript.

Place	Date	Hour	Summary of Events and Information	Remarks and references to Appendices
PHINC BOOM	1/3/17		Map Reference HAZEBROUCK and Belgium and France. Sheet 9 24. S.E. 1/20000 Training and recreational training. Lieut Col. R.C. Pratt D.S.O. rejoined from the Brigade Headquarters and took over command of Battalion.	MUA
	2/3/17		Training and Recreational training.	MUA
	3/3/17		Training and Recreational training.	MUA
	4/3/17		Divine Service.	MUA
	5/3/17		Training and Recreational training.	MUA
	6/3/17		The Battalion was inspected by the Brigadier General, Battalion Route March. Recreational training.	MUA
	7/3/17		Training and Recreational training.	MUA
	8/3/17		Training and Recreational training.	MUA
	9/3/17		Training and Recreational training.	MUA
	10/3/17		Training and Recreational training.	MUA
	11/3/17		Divine Service.	MUA
	12/3/17		Training and Recreational training. Transport joined Battalion in PHINCBOOM.	MUA
	13/3/17		Training and Recreational training.	MUA

WAR DIARY

of 11th (S) Batt R. Innes Killing Fusiliers

Army Form C. 2118.

INTELLIGENCE SUMMARY.
(Erase heading not required.)

March 1917

Place	Date	Hour	Summary of Events and Information	Remarks and references to Appendices
PRINC BOOM	14/3/17		Commanding Officer inspected Battalion at 11.15 a.m. Evening - Recreational training. D. Company reserves of Battalion Bath Competitions. Mill^r	
	15/3/17		Parties of Officers, other than Coy Comdrs. Recreational Training Mill^r	
	16/3/17		Battalion medically inspected. Training and Recreational Training. Mill^r	
	17/3/17		Divine Service. Mill^r	
	18/3/17		Training and Bathing. Lecture by Brigadier at S. METEREN, 6.0 p.m. to C.O.S and Company Commanders. Mill^r	
	19/3/17		Battalion left PRINC BOOM at 8.35 a.m. and marched via HAZEBROUCK to BLARINGHEM, arriving there at 1.6 p.m. Weather fine. Number of men falling out of ranks. NIL. Mill^r	
BLARINGHEM	21/3/17		Battalion left BLARINGHEM at 10.30 a.m. and marched via RACQUINGHEM, HAQUES and ST. OMER to ST. MARTIN-AU-LAERT, arriving there at 4.0 p.m. Weather bad - Snow Storms. No. of men falling out of ranks. 7. Mill^r	
MARTIN-AU-LAERT	22/3/17		Battalion left ST. MARTIN-AU-LAERT at 9.30.a.m., arriving at the following	

Army Form C. 2118.

WAR DIARY
or
INTELLIGENCE SUMMARY.
(Erase heading not required.)

March 1917. 2nd/11th/152 Batt R Inniskilling Fusiliers

Instructions regarding War Diaries and Intelligence Summaries are contained in F.S. Regs., Part II. and the Staff Manual respectively. Title pages will be prepared in manuscript.

Place	Date	Hour	Summary of Events and Information	Remarks and references to Appendices
ST. MARTIN-AU-LAERT	22/3/17	1.20 AM	Villages of Headquarters & C. Company WESTBECOURT. A & B Companies VAL-D'ACQUIN and D Company BOUVELINGHEM. Inspection of men falling out of route Mh.	JWS
WESTBECOURT	23/3/17		Conference at the disposal of O.C. Companies who made a thorough inspection of equipment.	JWS
VAL-D'ACQUIN	24/3/17		Training and Recreational training.	JWS
BOUVELINGHEM	25/3/17		Divine Service and Medical Inspection.	JWS
	26/3/17		Training. "B" Company proceeded to MISQUES and practised "The Attack."	JWS
	27/3/17		Training and Recreational training.	JWS
	28/3/17		"C" Company winners of Brigade Musketry Competition. "B" Company winners of Battalion Bayonet Fighting Competition.	JWS
	29/3/17		Training & recreational training. C Company to Raton, winners of Battalion Bombing competition. Weather fine.	JWS

WAR DIARY
or
INTELLIGENCE SUMMARY. 11th (S) Bn. R. Innis killing Fus.
(Erase heading not required)

Army Form C. 2118.

Remarks and references to Appendices

Place	Date	Hour	Summary of Events and Information
WESTRECOURT	30/3/17		Training and Recreational training. Brigade second in Brigade Signalling competition.
WAIL-DE-HAUOUN BOUVELINGHEM	31/3/17		Brigade Sports "Finals". Battalion Championship, tie between 11th (S) Bn. R. Innis. Fus. and 9th (S) Bn. R. Innis. Fus. No 6 Platoon "B" Coy. winners of Brigade Championship. No 6 Platoon "B" Coy. winners of Brigade Lewis Gun Championship. No 6 Platoon, winners of Brigade Bayonet Fighting Championship. No 4 Pltd 2 Runners of Brigade Bayonet F championship. No a3030 1/c Holmes E.C. Company runners of Brigade Featherweight Championship. Lance/Cpl ——— winners of Brigade Transport Championship. "C" Coy. winner of Brigade Middleweight Championship. 29520 Pte Robinson —— winner of Brigade S.B. Championship. Stretcher Bearers, runners up of Brigade Relay Race. Battalion Runners, runner up of Brigade Relay Race. Strength of Battalion 41 Officers. 726 other Ranks.

In the field.
W.C. Pratt Lieut. Col.
Comdg. 11 (S) Bn R Innis killing F.

CONFIDENTIAL.

W A R   D I A R Y

of

11th Battalion Royal Inniskilling Fusiliers,

from 1st April 1917
till 30th April 1917.

Army Form C. 2118.

WAR DIARY

of 1 ch (S) Batt. R. Inniskilling Fusrs.

April 1917.

Instructions regarding War Diaries and Intelligence Summaries are contained in F.S. Regs., Part II. and the Staff Manual respectively. Title pages will be prepared in manuscript.

(Erase heading not required.)

Place	Date	Hour	Summary of Events and Information	Remarks and references to Appendices
			Map Reference HAZEBROUCK S.a. and BELGIUM and France. Sheets 28. S.W. 2. 1/10,000. 28.S.W. 1/20,000.	
WESTBECOURT	1/4/17		Divine Service.	
	2/4/17		Training and Recreational Training. 2nd Lieut. H. Aylin joined from Cadet School.	
	3/4/17		Companies at disposal of O.C. Companies. (Snow Storm)	
	4/4/17		Battalion left WESTBECOURT at 7.45 a.m. and marched to ST. MARTIN-AU-LAERT. arriving there at 1.5. p.m. 5 men fell out on the line of march.	
ST-MARTIN-AU-LAERT.	5/4/17.		Battalion continued its march to HAZEBROUCK, leaving ST. MARTIN-AU-LAERT at 7 a.m. and arriving there at 3.55. p.m. No men fell out on march.	
HAZEBROUCK	6/4/17.		Battalion left HAZEBROUCK at 6.30. a.m. H.Q. and 2 Platoons of "B" Coy. proceeded to 3/4 mile N.W. of BAILLEUL, arriving there at 12.30. p.m., the remainder proceeded to Camp at KENNEL HILL. Transport and G.M. Stores situated in DRANOUTRE.	
KENNEL HILL	7/4/17		Battalion resting and bathed at DRANOUTRE.	
SPAN:BROEK LEFT SUB-SECTOR	8/4/17		Battalion relieved the 9th R. Irish Rifles in the SPANBROEK. LEFT SUB-SECTOR. "A" and "D" Coys in Front line, "C" Coy in Support and "B" Coy in Reserve. Relief completed at 10.45. p.m. Situation Normal.	

Army Form C. 2118.

WAR DIARY
of 11th (S) Batt. R. Irish Killing Fusrs.
April 1917.

INTELLIGENCE SUMMARY.
(Erase heading not required.)

Instructions regarding War Diaries and Intelligence Summaries are contained in F. S. Regs., Part II. and the Staff Manual respectively. Title pages will be prepared in manuscript.

Place	Date	Hour	Summary of Events and Information	Remarks and references to Appendices
SPANBROEK LEFT SUB-SECTOR	9/4/17		Situation normal. Draft of 4 arrives from Base.	
	10/4/17		Situation normal.	
	11/4/13		Companies carrying out inter company relief. Situation normal.	
	12/4/17		Situation normal.	
	13/4/17		Draft of 29 arrived from Base. Situation normal.	
	14/4/17		The Battalion were relieved in the trenches by the 10th R. Innis. Fus. Relief completed at 10.20 p.m. Battalion situated as follows :- "A", "B" Coys and 1 Platoon "D" Coy at Chateau, KEMMEL. 1 Platoon "D" Coy at Kemmel Dugouts, 2 Platoons "C" Coy at FORT EDWARD, 2 Platoons "C" Coy at "FORT REGINA" and Batt: H.Q. at CURES HOUSE, KEMMEL.	
KEMMEL	15/4/17		Drafts inspected by Commanding Officer. Medical Inspection and Working Parties. Draft training.	
	16/4/17		Working Parties and fatigues of "D" Coy called. Draft training.	
	17/4/17		Working Parties and 30 men of each Coy called. Draft of 3 men arrived. Draft training.	
	18/4/17		Working Parties and Batt: H.Q. called. Draft training.	

WAR DIARY

of F 11th (S) Batt. R. Inniskilling Fusiliers

Army Form C. 2118.

INTELLIGENCE SUMMARY

April 1917

(Erase heading not required.)

Instructions regarding War Diaries and Intelligence Summaries are contained in F.S. Regs., Part II. and the Staff Manual respectively. Title pages will be prepared in manuscript.

Place	Date	Hour	Summary of Events and Information	Remarks and references to Appendices
KEMMEL	19/4/17.		Working Parties &c.	
SPANBROEK RIGHT SUB-SECTOR	20/4/17.		The Battalion relieved the 9th (S) Batt. R. Inniskilling Fusrs. in the SPANBROEK, RIGHT SUB-SECTOR. "A" and "D" Coys in the Front Line, "C" Coy in Support and "B" Coy in Reserve. Artillery bombarded enemy's 1st and 2nd Lines and pineapple from 12 midnight to 5.30 a.m. Strong.	
	21/4/17.		Situation Normal. Snipers	
	22/4/17.		Situation Normal. Snipers	
	23/4/17.		Companies carried out an inter-Company relief. Situation Normal Snipers	
	24/4/17.		Situation Normal. Snipers.	
	25/4/17.		Casualties - Sgt Harps J. and Pte Henders J. wounded. Situation Normal Snipers Casualties - Pte's Richards G.H. and Mann, R. Killed. The Battalion	
KEMMEL	26/4/17.		were relieved in the RIGHT SUB-SECTOR by the 10th (S) Batt. R. Inniskilling Fusrs. and went back to Brigade Support at KEMMEL. "C" and "D" Coys at Chateau, KEMMEL. "B" Coy in FORT REGINA, 2 Platoons of FORT ~~~~~~ EDWARD "B" Coy at FORT ~~~~~~ B Coy. at KEMMEL DUGOUTS. Our artillery bombarded Enemy's lines from R.E.	

WAR DIARY of 11th (S) Batt. R. Inniskilling Fusiliers

Army Form C. 2118.

INTELLIGENCE SUMMARY.

April 1917.

Place	Date	Hour	Summary of Events and Information	Remarks and references to Appendices
KEMMEL	26/4/17.			
	27/4/17.	5.30 p.m.	Relief completed at 10.25 p.m. MM3. Battalion resting and fitting out. MM3	
	28/4/17.		Working parties position. Transport called. Casualties in KEMMEL VILLAGE. Ptes. Lorimer, Bucket, Wright & Henderson Wounded. MM3	
	29/4/17.		Divine Service. Our artillery bombarded the enemy's lines and points during the day, enemy's retaliation becoming increasingly aggressive. Between 12 noon and 5 P.m. over 50 shells were fired in KEMMEL VILLAGE. Casualties Pte Meanon G. wounded. Captain F.C. Mowbray proceeded to join 2nd Divn Army (Special Reserve) and struck off the strength of Battalion. Lieut G.M.F. Irvine took over command of "C" Company. MM3	
	30/4/17.		Working parties. Bathing arrangements MM3. The undermentioned have been awarded the "Water Divisional Card" for gallantry during raid on enemy's trenches: 14084 C.S.M. W.R. Lawrie. 17378 a/Sergt. R. Luyton. 11511 Cpl. W. McComb. 14478 Sgt. Nesbitt. 15336 Sgt. H. White	

Army Form C. 2118.

WAR DIARY
or
INTELLIGENCE SUMMARY.
(Erase heading not required.)

April 1917. 11th (S) Batt. R. Innis. Fuslrs.

Place	Date	Hour	Summary of Events and Information	Remarks and references to Appendices
In the Field	30th April 1917.		19726 Cpl. J. Donaldson. 11745 L/Cpl. J. Keys. 14031. L/Cpl. J. Cairns. 18767. L/Cpl. J. Lynch. 16245. L/Cpl. S. Johnstone. 18315. Pte. H. Gardiner. 14729 Pte. G. Rutherford 16831. Pte. G. Moore. 14056 Pte. J. Clement. 15236 Pte. M. Hutchinson. 14025 Pte. J.H. Bones. M.M. Strength of Battalion 40 Officers 934 other ranks. M.M. A.C.Pratt. Lieut-Col., Comdg. 11th (S). Batt. R. Inniskilling Fuslrs.	

CONFIDENTIAL.

WAR DIARY

OF

11TH. BATTALION ROYAL INNISKILLING FUSILIERS,

FROM 1ST. MAY, 1917.

TILL 31ST. MAY, 1917.

WAR DIARY or INTELLIGENCE SUMMARY

Army Form C. 2118.

May 1917 — 7/1st (9) Bn R Inniskilling Fus

(Erase heading not required.)

Instructions regarding War Diaries and Intelligence Summaries are contained in F. S. Regs., Part II. and the Staff Manual respectively. Title pages will be prepared in manuscript.

Place	Date	Hour	Summary of Events and Information	Remarks and references to Appendices
SPANBROEK LEFT SUB SECTOR	1/5/17 2/5/17		West Flanders BELGIUM and FRANCE Sheet 28 SW 1/20000. Strength 40 officers 939 other ranks. Working parties and Ration Battalion relieved the 9th (S) Bn R. Innis Killing Fusiliers in the SPANBROEK left Sub Sector "A" and "D" Coys in Front line, "B" Coy Left Spt "C" Coy right Spt, "C" Coy Right Spt. One gas alarm was sounded about 10.15 p.m. but no signs of Gas were seen.	Warm Warm
	3/5/17		Situation normal.	Warm
	4/5/17		Situation normal. Large fire was seen behind enemy's line about 8.30 p.m. Corrections 14636 Pte Toland S. killed and 14120 C/O Simpson R. wounded	Warm
	5/5/17		Situation normal. Companies carried out inter-company reliefs. 16846 Pte Moore T. wounded.	Warm
	6/5/17		Situation normal.	Warm
	7/5/17		Situation normal.	Warm
	8/5/17		A dummy raid was carried out to induce the enemy to expose themselves at 11.30 a.m. and 2 T.M. opened onto our Front Line Support and	Warm

WAR DIARY of 1st Can 50 Batt D.R. Quinchillery Coy

Army Form C. 2118.

May 1917

INTELLIGENCE SUMMARY.

(Erase heading not required.)

Instructions regarding War Diaries and Intelligence Summaries are contained in F.S. Regs., Part II. and the Staff Manual respectively. Title pages will be prepared in manuscript.

Place	Date	Hour	Summary of Events and Information	Remarks and references to Appendices
SPRINGROEK LEFT	8/5/17		Communication trenches SPRINGROEK-NIEUK, at ¾ aim D from the canal and during Byrnes which were out in NO MANS LAND night previous were killed at by news of our own. Two of the enemy were seen running outward from the front line at N.30.9.50 and one rifle day was appeared to have been blown in. Relation was magnificent. The Battalion were relieved in the trenches by the 1st (S) Batt R. Quinchillery Fusilier and went back to Brigade Support. Battalion H.Q. at Curlo House, KEMMEL. A and B Coys at Claram. KEMMEL, C Coy KEMMEL BEEHIVES, D Coy 2 Platoons at FORT REGINA and 2 Platoons at FORT ENYARD.	
KEMMEL	9/5/17		Battalion resting and fitting out. Bathing.	WDAM
	10/5/17		Working parties and Commanding Officers Inspection dress of T.O.R.	WDAM
	11/5/17		Working parties and Bathing.	WDAM
	12/5/17		Casualties 436653 Pte Potter W.J. Wounded and G.17373 Pte Potts G. Wounded Pte Potts since died of wounds.	WDAM WDAM

Army Form C. 2118.

WAR DIARY
or
INTELLIGENCE SUMMARY.

May 1917.

(Erase heading not required.)

Instructions regarding War Diaries and Intelligence Summaries are contained in F. S. Regs., Part II. and the Staff Manual respectively. Title pages will be prepared in manuscript.

Place	Date	Hour	Summary of Events and Information	Remarks and references to Appendices
KEMMEL	13/5/17		Some Sports and working parties.	WDM
WINCHELL HUTS DOMINION HUTS 14/5/17			The Battalion were relieved in Brigade Support by the 13th Royal Scots Rifles and went back to Dominion Reserve Huts at A.9.d. & HUTCHARD HUTS and 9 companies to KEMMEL Huts N.25.d. 60, 70. Lieut W.E. Lyles struck off strength.	
	15/5/17		Working parties and bathing.	WDM
	16/5/17		Working parties, bathing and Specialists training	WDM
	17/5/17		Working parties and Bathing.	WDM
	18/5/17		Working parties and Bathing.	WDM
	19/5/17		Working parties.	WDM
	20/5/17		Working parties. 2nd Lieut C.H. Stoley accepted for Commission in R.Div. army and D struck off	WDM
	21/5/17		Working parties	WDM
	22/5/17		Working parties.	WDM

Army Form C. 2118.

WAR DIARY
of 11th (S) Batt. R. Inniskilling Fus.rs
INTELLIGENCE SUMMARY.

(Erase heading not required.)

Instructions regarding War Diaries and Intelligence Summaries are contained in F.S. Regs., Part II. and the Staff Manual respectively. Title pages will be prepared in manuscript.

May, 1917

Place	Date	Hour	Summary of Events and Information	Remarks and references to Appendices
WAKEFIELD HUTS DRANOUTRE	23/5/17		Working parties.	10/Am
	24/5/17		Working parties and Bathing. Draft of 12 arrives from Base.	10/Am
	25/5/17		Working parties.	10/Am
	26/5/17		Working parties.	10/Am
	27/5/17		Divine Service and working parties.	10/Am
	28/5/17		Working parties. No 43627 Pte Cox. C wounded by shell fire.	10/Am
	29/5/17		Working parties. Draft of 5 O.R. arrives from Base.	10/Am
	30/5/17		Working parties and bathing	10/Am
	31/5/17		Working parties and bathing	10/Am
			Strength of Battalion. 36 officers 928. O.R.	10/Am

In the Field
31st May 1917.

W.L._____ Col.
Comdg. 11th (S) Batt R. Inniskilling Fus.rs

Vol 21

WAR DIARY FOR MONTH OF JUNE 1917.
—o—o—o—o—o—o—o—o—o—o—o—o—o—o—o—o—

11TH. ROYAL INNISKILLING FUSILIERS.
—o—o—o—o—o—o—o—o—o—o—o—o—

CONFIDENTIAL.

ORIGINAL.

WAR DIARY
of the

11th (SERVICE) BATTALION ROYAL INNISKILLING FUSILIERS.

FROM 1st. JUNE, 1917.   TO 30th JUNE, 1917.

(VOLUME XXI)

WAR DIARY or INTELLIGENCE SUMMARY

Army Form C. 2118.

June 1917 2nd (S) Batt. R. Inniskilling Fus.

Place	Date	Hour	Summary of Events and Information	Remarks and references to Appendices
DRANOUTRE	1/6/17		Map reference HAZEBROUCK 5.B. BELGIUM and FRANCE. Sheet 28. S.W. 1/20000 Battalion H.Q. and Transport moved from WAKEFIELD HUTS (J.27. S.E. 1/40000 Sheet No.28.) C.O. when comfortably settled in huts and bivouacs. Remainder of Battalion on working parties. Casualties: 2 other ranks wounded by shell fire.	Mur
MONT NOIR	2/6/17		Coy working parties and the exception of 2 Platoons formed the Reserve at them now camp, other two Platoons in working parties at KEMMEL Hill. Under the command of Lieut. F. Bar. F.R.S. Dean M.C.	
"	3/6/17		Reinforcement Draft of 1 Officer 2/Lieut. Hendley. Lieut. W. Dill Sm[ith] at Artillery Transport.	Mur
"	4/6/17		W. Dill Training on general line of attack on Artillery demonstration Ground. Still from to Brig.	Mur
"	5/6/17		W. Dill Training and practice attack going out with accessories for attack. Heavy Enemy barrage all night 4/5.	Mur
			1st and 2nd Battalion moved from new camp at M.20.a.6.6. to WAKEFIELD HUTS arriving there at 10.30 a.m. Then rested and slept until 5 p.m. Dinner Served at 7 p.m. Battalion moved to Assembly trenches SOMBROEK SECTOR being WAKEFIELD HUTS at 9.30 p.m. (1st Platoon) relief completed at 2.16. a.m. Zero 3.10 a.m.	
WAKEFIELD HUTS	6/6/17		Men not called on for PECAUTRA MINE left a crater zero 2.15. 3 a.m. in advance and 20 feet deep Artillery open what had been intermittent all the also came down on Enemy trenches from Line 2.10 seconds after Zero. Battalion was advanced to attack in 4th Waves Second	
SOMBROEK SECTOR				Mur

WAR DIARY
INTELLIGENCE SUMMARY

June 1917. 1/4 (5) BN P Something Fus[?]

Army Form C. 2118.

(Erase heading not required.)

Place	Date	Hour	Summary of Events and Information	Remarks and references to Appendices
BLUE LINE	7/6/17		2 DAY Casualties - Killed 3 Officers and 15 other ranks. Wounded 6 Officers and 85 other ranks. Sent off wounded 3 other ranks. Sgd.	
SPANBROEK SECTOR	9/6/17		Battalion was relieved by 1/5 R.W.F. and moved to WAKEFIELD HUTS SHEET 28 N.W.I. Orders received to proceed to WAKEFIELD HUTS early next day. Shout 9.30 pm our artillery bombarded enemy lines between trenches N.7 N.8 and N.9 FIELDEN LANE N.I.2 on new enemy front line. Sgd.	
WAKEFIELD HUTS	9/6/17		Battalion moved back to WAKEFIELD HUTS. Officers and Warrant Officers in HOD Shout marching hits on WQS and L.Cpls to their movement. Rejoined units 16.95 O.S. 7th Lans. Commanded MCDNILE MULTIPLE and Lieuts. COD Harry and J Snout Off 9.Six. placements on the 2 Dan Bay. Sgd.	
	10/6/17		Commanding Officer went to F[?] GUNNER Sgd.	
	11/6/17		Inspection of KIG and Equipment Sgd.	
	12/6/17		Whole morning Company Officers inspect of L.C Company. Sgd.	
			Remainder of day spent at inspect of Regt if 3 arms. Sgd.	
HUNT. N6.18	13/6/17		The Battalion less transport forward at N.30. N.S. and shipped to 1st Canadian Something for the night. Transport moved to reentry of MRR.MRIB Ref a. a. 5. Sgd.	

2449 Wt. W14957/M90 750,000 1/16 J.B.C. & A. Forms/C.2118/12.

WAR DIARY or INTELLIGENCE SUMMARY

Army Form C. 2118.

June 1917 — 1/1st (S) Bn R. Dublin Fus.

Place	Date	Hour	Summary of Events and Information	Remarks and references to Appendices
NUIT NOIR	13/6/17		EXTRACT FROM LONDON GAZETTE. Wounded on 27/5/17. Capt R.W. Knight. 2nd Lieut J.S. Child. 6224 Sgt. R. Reed. D.Co.	
	14/6/17		Working parties.	
	15/6/17		Working parties.	
	16/6/17		Shooting practice. Range.	
	17/6/17		Divine Service. Lieut 10th Regiment 2nd Lt S.D.N. Harrison joined for duty. Orders received to move to SOUCHEZ area 2.30 a.m. 18 inst. Battalion formed + left for area.	
SOUCHEZ FARM	18/6/17		LITTLEST FARM. 11.10 a.m. 'D' Co. 'B' Co. Battalion relieved 10th Royal Warwick Regt out Gr. Lancaster	
COSTA WEAR SUB SECTOR	19/6/17		Regt in the COSTSVILLE LEFT SUB SECTOR. Strength 12.45 a.s 6. OR. 257. OR. Transport + Details turned to LOST FARM HQ + QM Sheltrs. Battalion party formed on 8th Shelter. Casualty 1 O.R. wounded. Gr.	
	20/6/17		Shelter turned. Enemy trench mortars. Casualty 1 O.R. wounded. Gr.	
	21/6/17		Shelter turned. Enemy turned. Trench mortar notification received from 10th Sqn R.E. Elms. 5 sets if enemy S.O.S	
	22/6/17		2nd Lt Q.A. Bailey out sick — Lt of B.Coy wounded 9.45 a.m. Sniper round S.B. on duty.	
	23/6/17		Another Shot + E.M + Spare round Shelter turned.	

Army Form C. 2118.

WAR DIARY
or
INTELLIGENCE SUMMARY

(Erase heading not required.)

June 1917. 1st Bn. R. Inniskilling Fus.

Place	Date	Hour	Summary of Events and Information	Remarks and references to Appendices
OOSTTAVERNE SUB SECTOR	24/6/17		Battalion now relieved in front line trenches by 14th R. Irish Rifles. Relief and move back carried out without incident. Casualties 5 other ranks wounded. 2nd Lt. J. Carlile joined for duty.	nil
SUPPORT TRENCHES	25/6/17		Stokes mortar activity. Enemy trench mortars.	nil
"	26/6/17		Shelter normal. Nothing to report.	
"	27/6/17		Situation normal. Nothing to report. Enemy T.M.s & Whizz-bangs active.	nil
GARDEN FARM	28/6/17		Battalion now moved up to relief Middlesex Regt. in the OOSTTAVERNE LEFT SUB SECTOR. Battalion relieved by Tanks and Stores now accommodated in GARDEN FARM, M.34.78. Casualties 1 other rank wounded.	nil
"	29/6/17		Battalion resting and fitting up. Re-equipment. Draft of 2 O.Rs sent out to other Tanks Funnel.	Entr nil
"	30/6/17		Battalion moved to STRAZEELE area, arriving there at 2.25 a.m. Heavy shower.	nil
			Strength of Battalion in 30 Officers 814 O. Ranks	nil

In the Field
1st July 1917

A. C. Pratt
Lieut - Col
Comdg "1st(?)" Bn. R. Inniskilling Fus.

11th (S) BATTN. ROYAL INNISKILLING FUSILIERS.

SPECIAL ORDER OF THE DAY

The Commanding Officer, on the eve of the Offensive, wishes to express to every Officer, N.C.O. and man of the Battalion, his appreciation of the way in which they have worked, willingly and wholeheartedly, in the interests of the cause. He has the most thorough confidence that the Honour of their King and Country, and of the Regiment to which they have the honour to belong, will be upheld most honourably through all difficulties and dangers which may come in our way.

He wishes every Officer, N.C.O. and man, GOD SPEED and THE BEST OF LUCK as they go over the top.

(sgd) A.C. PRATT. Lieut-Col.
Commanding 11th (S) Battn. Royal Inniskilling Fusiliers.

IN THE FIELD,
6th June 1917.

11th (S) BATTN. ROYAL INNISKILLING FUSILIERS.

CASUALTIES.
7th June 1917.

Captain Henry GALLAUGHER, D.S.O.	Killed.
2nd.Lieut. J.G.ROBERTSON.	do.
2nd.Lieut. G.PEAK-GARLAND.	do.
Captain G.M.FORDE.	Wounded.
2nd.Lieut.J.R.M.HANNA.	do.
2nd.Lieut.W.J.C.TUNSTALL.	do.
2nd.Lieut. S.PATTERSON.	do.
2nd.Lieut.H.ANGLISS.	do.
2nd.Lieut. W.M.H.STEWART,	do.
2nd.Lieut. J.J.KENNEDY.	do.

15 Other Ranks	Killed.
4 " "	Died of wounds.
84 " "	Wounded.

(sgd) A.C.PRATT. Lieut-Col.
Commanding 11th (S) Battn.Rl.Inniskilling Fusiliers.

WAR DIARY.

NARRATIVE OF OPERATIONS IN ATTACK ON ENEMY POSITION on 7th June 1917.

1. **UNIT.**

    11th Service Battalion Royal Inniskilling Fusiliers.
    Commanded by Lieut-Col. A.C.Pratt, D.S.O.

2. **ATTACHMENTS.**

    "D" Company, 11th Battalion Royal Irish Rifles (Moppers up) under Command of Captain Somers.

    4 Machine Guns of 109th Machine Gun Company under Command of Lieutenants Root and Bowerbank.

    1 Stokes Mortar Gun of 109th Trench Mortar Battery under Command of Second Lieutenant Towden.

    Liasion Officers.   Artillery.   2nd. Lieut.Reynolds
                                         105th Batt. R.F.A.
                        Intelligence.   Lieut.Dunne
                                         6th Bn.R.Irish Regiment.

3. **ORDER OF BATTLE.**   Boundaries and Objectives.

    As shewn on attached Map whilst in Assembly Trenches at ZERO.

    "B" Company, (Captain H.Gallagher, D.S.O.)on right forming first wave, with 1 Platoon 11th R.Irish Rifles (Moppers up) supported by "A" Company, (Captain W.M.Knight).On the left "C" Company (acting Captain S.Finke) with 2 Platoons 11th R.Ir. Rifles (Moppers up) supported by "D" Company (Captain G.M.Forde M.C.)

4. **PLAN.**

    "B" and "C" Companies led the attack to "RED LINE" NAPIES RESERVE our FIRST Objective where "A" and "D" Companies leapfrogged through to SECOND Objective "BLUE LINE" where 9th Battalion Royal Inniskilling Fusiliers leapfrogged through to "BLACK LINE" on far side of WYSCHAETE

5. **ACCOUNT OF THE ACTION.**

    2.30 A.M. The Battalion was formed up in Assembly Trenches.

    3.10.a.m. ZERO. Mines exploded in our front. PECKHAM MINE left a Crater some 80 yards diameter and 30 feet deep. Artillery fire, which had been intermittent up to this, came down in barrage on Enemy's front line.

    Twenty seconds after ZERO Battalion was deploying for attack in "NO MAN'S LAND" and reached enemy's front line as barrage lifted. From this point, they followed closely on Artillery Barrage to their final objective "BLUE LINE". Meeting with only slight opposition arrived at scheduled time of ZERO plus 100.- and consolidated.

6. **COMMENTS.**

    (a) Artillery Barrage.

    The Artillery Barrage was magnificent throughout and by following it up closely, the Infantry were enabled to mop up all enemy strong points without any serious opposition. In one or two cases where the enemy trenches had not been properly broken up, there was some slight resistance, but a few picked rifle shots and Rifle Grenadiers with an occasional burst of Lewis Gun fire were sufficient to quell all resistance.

    Our only difficulty was to prevent men running into the Barrage. In many cases we were only 30 yards behind the Barrage and 50 yards always proved a safe distance.

continued.

(a) Enemy Barrage.
With the exception of a barrage for 10 minutes on some of our RESERVE trenches, enemy's barrage was negligible.

(b) Enemy Machine Guns.
Never really had any chance to get going, one caused some slight trouble on our right, but was silenced by a Lewis Gun and some Rifle Bombers without delay.
One enemy Machine Gunner is reported to have been found chained to his gun, at any rate his captor, not being able to free him from the gun, put the muzzle of his rifle against the chain and fired it, thus cutting the chain. this, however, was the only instance of a man being chained to a gun that we saw.

(d) Wire.
All wire was cut in shreds, not merely gaps, and caused absolutely no obstacle.

(e) Tanks.
The tanks advancing over ground absolutely covered with shell holes, were unable to reach us before we gained our objective nor was their assistance required, as the enormous volume of artillery fire was most accurate and sustained.

(f) Aeroplanes.
Contact aeroplanes flew over us, we indicated our position to them by flares with success.

(g) Information.
Message cards with rough outlined maps printed on them, were much used in sending back information. For the transmission of Intelligence, Runners, Visual and on two occasions Pigeons, were used. We were enabled to send back messages by telephone from Brigade forward Station about NAPIER SUPPORT within an hour of entering enemy's lines.

7. MISCELLANEOUS.
Rifle and Lewis Gun fire were both used and in one instance a Machine Gun was silenced by Rifle Grenades.
Flags for identification were found useful.
The chief lesson which we learnt was the necessity of keeping up close to the Artillery Barrage, but at the same time the danger of troops running into our own barrage is common, and due to keenness this happened to us on two occasions.
The simpler and straighter the barrage can be laid out, the better as the changes of direction are difficult with troops eager to press on to the attack.

A. C. Pratt.
Lieut-Col:
Comg. 11th (S) Bn. R.Inniskilling Fusiliers.

IN THE FIELD

14th June 1917

11th (S) BATTN. ROYAL INNISKILLING FUSILIERS.

SPECIAL ORDER OF THE DAY

The Commanding Officer desires to place on record his appreciation of the manner in which the attack on the Enemy's position at WYTSCHAETE was carried out on the 7th.inst. and the many deeds of gallantry that were performed, the result of which was that the Battalion carried each objective ordered, and consolidated the position taken, with the added result of nearly 200 prisoners, 2 Machine Guns and 1 Field Gun.

The Commander-in-Chief, who viewed the operations, has already expressed his commendation of the work done by the Division in the attack.

While deploring the loss of our gallant comrades who have fallen in the fight, he feels convinced that the noble example of self-sacrifice set by such as Captain H.GALLAUGHER, D.S.O. who, although severely wounded, continued to fight on, will set us all an example of how a true Soldier can meet his death fighting for his King and Country and adding fresh honour to the laurels already won by this Battalion. His life and gallant end is an example to us of the true spirit of continuing to fight on until this War is satisfactorily concluded.

(sgd) A.C.PRATT. Lieut-Col.
Commanding 11th (S) Battn.Royal Inniskilling Fusiliers.

IN THE FIELD,
    8th June 1917.

Army Form W. 3121.

Date of Recommendation. 13th June 1917.

Schedule No. (to be left blank)	Unit	Regtl. No.	Rank and Name	Action for which commended	Recommended by	Honour or Reward	(To be left blank)
	11th (S) Battn. Royal Inniskilling Fusiliers.		Captain Henry GALLAUGHER, D.S.O.	On the 7th June 1917, in the SPANBROEK Sector on the occasion of the general attack on the MESSINES – WYTSCHAETE Ridge. This Officer was severely wounded before he reached the enemy first line, his left arm being broken. He threw down the rifle which he was carrying -- slung on his left shoulder and said "That's all right boys I'll do well with a revolver. He continued to lead his men in the attack, stopping them when they got too close to our artillery barrage and giving his commands as cooly as if on parade and as if he had never been wounded. He led them to their final objective but just as his position which he had gained was being consolidated, he fell mortally wounded. His bravery has never been in doubt, he was the idol of his men and of the Battalion in general, and wherever he led his men would follow. His example on all occasions and on this day in particular remain an example which will always be treasured in this Battalion.	(Sgd) A.C.PRATT Lieut-Col. Comdg.11th (S) Battn.R.Inniskilling Fusrs.	V.C.	

109th Infantry Brigade. 36th (ULSTER) Division. IXth Corps.

11th (S) BATTN. ROYAL INNISKILLING FUSILIERS.

RECOMMENDATIONS FOR IMMEDIATE REWARD IN ORDER OF MERIT.

	Recommended for
Captain H. GALLAUGHER, D.S.O. (Killed in action)	V.C. (posthumous)
Captain W.M. KNIGHT.	D.S.O.
Captain G.M. FORDE.	BAR TO M.C.
Acting Captain S. FLUKE	M.C.
2nd. Lieut. W.J.C. TUNSTALL,	M.C.
Captain Rev. A. SPENCE. (Chaplain C. of L. attached)	M.C.

OTHER RANKS.

No. 8893 Sergt GREAVES, J.	D.C.M.
" 14481 " PARKE, J.	D.C.M.
" 14058 Corpl EDWARDS, J.R.	M.M.
" 14895 L/Cpl MUIR, W.	M.M.
" 18315 L/Sgt GARDNER, W.	M.M.
" 9860 Sergt OWENS, R.J.	M.M.
" 14091 " McCLINTOCK, R.	M.M.
" 43069 Pte GARRITY, A.	M.M.
" 29097 " MEHKE, J.	M.M.
" 28980 " McGEE, P.	M.M.
" 16828 " BEATTY, J.R.	M.M.
" 17245 L/Cpl McCLINTOCK, T.	M.M.

A.C. PRATT.   Lieut-Col.
Commanding 11th (S) Bn. Rl. Inniskilling Fusiliers.

IN THE FIELD,
  14th June 1917.

SCOUTS.
Green Armlet. Same as Runner and in addition Field Glasses.

CARRYING
PARTIES.

O.C. Companies will each detail 1 Platoon (less Lewis Gun Section) as Carriers. One third of these carriers will follow the fourth wave.

Two thirds of them will remain at Battalion Headquarters at N.29.a.40.90 and will be under the Command of 2nd. Lt. R.S. Dream M.C. assisted by Sergt. Storey, and 2 caretakers now in charge of the Battalion Dump.

Carriers loads will be as under, and 3 Yukon Packs per Company will be kept continually employed for carrying:—

  Water 3 Petrol Tins 66 lbs.
  25 Sandbags, 2 Rolls Barbed Wire 70 lbs
  3 Boxes Bombs 60 lbs
  25 Sandbags, 7 Shovels 2 Picks. 61 lbs.

The attention of O.C. Company's and Platoon Commanders is specially directed to S.S. 135 (Instruction for training Division for offensive action) Pages 54 & 55

28. RALLYING POSTS.

The Battalion Rallying post will be Battalion Headquarters. Any unwounded man becoming detached from his Platoon and unable to rejoin it should find his way to the Battalion Rallying Post. Carrying parties will also be based on this post, so that there will always be an Officer on the spot to deal with parties of men who have reported.

2nd Lt. R.S. Dream M.C. will be in charge of the post.

29. STOKES MORTARS.

One Stokes Mortar and Crew will be attached to the Battalion. This gun however will come under the orders of Officer Commanding 9th (S) Bn. Rl. Inniskilling Fusiliers, for the capture of the GREEN LINE and BLACK LINE when this Battalion leap-frogs.

(Sgd) A. C. PRATT, LIEUT COL
Comdg. 11th (S) Bn. Rl. Inniskilling Fusrs.

Copy No 1 O.C. 11th Innis: Fusrs Copy No 8 Signalling Officer
  2 O.C. 6th R. Irish Regt.   9 Intelligence Officer
  3 O.C. 11th R. Irish Rifles.   10 Quartermaster.
  4 O.C. "A" Company   11 File
  5 O.C. "B" Company   12 War Diary.
  6 O.C. "C" Company
  7 O.C. "D" Company.

Watches will be synchronised at... ... ...
It is essential to have a RELIABLE watch.

The Battalion is responsible for the Capture
of BLUE LINE and for the present of O.P.'s and ...
The junction of NAPLES AVENUE & KEMMEL WYTSCHAETE ROAD
will be formed as a strong point and will be known as
S.P. 4.   The junction of NAP RESERVE & KEMMEL WYTSCHAETE
ROAD will be formed as a strong point and will be known
as S.P. 9.   These strong points are to be made es-
pecially for flank defence.
    Our R.R.Dump is moved to N.29.c.45.80.
    O.C.Company's must settle how many Dumps and
where they will have them in the enemy lines, for ammunition, tools, water etc.
    12 Yukon Packs are being served out to the
Battalion. 3 will be given to each Company.
    The Carrying Platoons of each Company will be
the last Wave of the Company.
    The necessity of eventually getting up a good a... ...
of wire is absolutely important—wiring is more important than digging—a good belt of wire is invaluable.

DRESS AND EQUIPMENT

RIFLEMAN

Equipment, Rifle, bayonet, 120 rounds S.A.A.
2 No. 5 Mills Grenades, 2 Sandbags, 2 day haversack,
full water bottle, Field dressing, capsules. IN PACK
Cap Tin and cover, waterproof sheet, cardigan, Iron
rations, unexpired portion of day's rations and next
days rations. Haversack ration(Ration 2) 2 oranges
chewing gum, candle, matches, solidified alcohol.
    One man in every section carries in addition
One pair of pliers. One man with clippers and hedging
gloves, this man to wear a piece of black cloth on his
shoulder strap. One man wire nippers on rifle.   At
least 50% Carry Wires.

BOMBER (Thrower)

As RIFLEMAN, but 50 rounds of ammunition instead of 120.   In addition he carries 6 bombs, 2 in
the pouch and 4 in bomb bag hooked on to right side of
his belt.

CARRIER in the Rifle bomb Squad.

Same as the Thrower but carries 2 bombs in
pouch, and 12 bombs in bomb bucket.

BAYONET MAN

Same as rifleman.

RIFLE GRENADIER.

Same as rifleman but 50 rounds of ammunition
instead of 120.   In addition he carries 10 Rifle
Grenades.

LEWIS GUNNER No 1 and 2.

Lewis Gun, Haversack, and 30 rounds of
revolver ammunition. Pack same as rifleman.

REMAINDER OF LEWIS GUN TEAM

Same as RIFLEMAN but 50 rounds S.A.A.
instead of 120. In addition each carries 6 magazines
in two carriers.

MOPPING UP

Same as rifleman, and 2 "P" or "P.G.P." bombs
to be carried in Pack until reaching position from
which they are going to Mop Up. (for "B" and "C" Coy.)
and Rifle for "A" and "D" Companies Coy. Also 1 p's ...

SNIPERS and Scouts. Same as rifle on but 50
rounds of ammunition instead of 120, No sandbags.

RUNNERS: Rear look and Pencil in right hand over
                jacket.
SCOUTS: Green Armlet.
                Same as Runner and in addition Field Glasses.

CARRIERS.   Yellow Armlets.
                S.A.A. Carriers as Rifleman but 50 rounds of
                S.A.A. and 2 bombs in pouches - carried in bandolier
                crosswise 5 bandoliers of ammunition over each
                shoulder.
                        No 5(III) Grenade Carriers, as S.A.A.
                carriers but instead of 5 bandoliers 12 bombs, making
                a total of 20 bombs and 12 bombs to be carried in a
                bomb bucket.
                        Rifle Grenade Carriers, as S.A.A.Carriers
                but instead of 5 bandoliers S.A.A. 15 Rifle Grenades No 20
                or 20 Rifle Grenades.
                CARRIERS OF WATER. (Inflated Water). As S.A.Carriers
                but instead of 5 bandoliers S.A.A. 1 petrol tin of
                water carried in Pack - the articles enumerated to be
                carried in Pack are to be carried in the Haversack.
                CARRIERS SANDBAGS   As S.A.A Carriers but instead of
                5 bandoliers 20 Sandbags and 1(Shovel).
                CARRIERS TOOLS   As S.A.A. Carriers but instead of 5
                bandoliers 1 pick carrier 4 pack and 1 shovel.
                LEWIS GUN MAGAZINE CARRIERS   same as Rifleman but 50
                rounds S.A.A. carried by men in addition each carries
                4 Magazines in Haversack.

                        NUMBER OF CARRIERS PER COMPANY
                Lewis Gun Magazine   2   Water Carriers   4
                S.A.A.   4   Sandbag Carriers 4
                No 5 Grenades   8   Tool Carriers (pick)2
                Rifle Grenades   2   "   Shovels 4

DUTIES   To be detailed by O.C. Companies probably
(LEFT TO COY.H.Q. as) CARRIED RESERVE.

Secret   War Diary   Copy No. 11

OPERATION ORDER NO. [?]
by
LIEUT-COL A. C. PRATT, D.S.O.
COMMANDING 11th (S) Bn. R. INNISKILLING FUSILIERS.

1. BOUNDARIES. Right and left boundary as previously indicated and drawn in on Maps.
Boundaries between Companies are our line N 30 a 30. 97 Enemy line N 30a 72. 90 MAP ALLEY to MAPLE SUPPORT inclusive to Right Company, thence by N 30 b 15. 95, thence to N. 24. d. 75. 10', 0. 19. c. 02. 20. MAP AVENUE inclusive to Right Company., MAP RESERVE to left Company to O.19.c. 43. 29.

2. COMMUNICATION TRENCHES. Communication Trenches for IN and OUT Traffic will be as follows:--
IN trenches   QUEEN'S GATE
                           THREE K's LANE.

OUT trenches,   PALL MALL
                           SHEPHERD'S LANE.
                           REGENT STREET.

3. HEADQUARTERS.
BRIGADE H.Q.   N.29.c.50.45
BATTALION H.Q.   N.29.c.40.90.
14th R. IRISH RIFLES H.Q.   N.29.c.70.80.
LEFT FLANK BATTN. H.Q.   N.23.c.67.75.(Irish House)

4. FORMATION. The Battalion(with 1 Company 14th R.Irish Rifles, as moppers up,) will attack with two Companies in the front line "B" on the right "C" on the left with two Companies in support, "A" on the right, "D" on the left. Each Company will supply one Platoon less Lewis Gun Team as Carriers.

5. OBJECTIVES
1st Objective RED line
2nd   "   BLUE line
3rd   "   GREEN line
4th   "   BLACK line.

6. TIME TABLE The leading waves go over the parapet at ZERO and the times of arrival at and lift of barrage from the successive lines are as follows:--

	Arrive	Depart
	0	4
NAPLES TRENCH,	20	69
Red line	100	224
Blue line	250	264
Green line		

7. ASSEMBLY Front Line and Support line Ketchen Avenue to N.30.a.00.60.

8. ATTACK The Battalion will Attack on a four Platoon front in four waves.

1st WAVE On the Right 2 Platoons of "B" Company, with 1 Platoon of 14th R. Irish Rifles, as moppers up.
On the left 2 Platoons "C" Company, with 2 Platoons 14th R. Irish Rifles, as Moppers up

2nd WAVE On the Right 2 Platoons "B"Company on the left 2 Platoons "C" Company.

3rd WAVE On the right 2 Platoons "A" Company on the left 2 Platoons "D" Company.

4th WAVE On the right 2 Platoons "A" Company, on the left 2 Platoons "D" Company.

The Battalion will take the Red and Blue lines the Attack will be "leap frog" "B" and [?] Companies taking the Red line and "A" and "D" Companies the

Blue Line

The 9th Batln. Royal Inniskilling Fusiliers will pass through the Battalion on the blue line to take the next objective Green line

                                                           Hrs. Mins.
TIMINGS   Leave our line at Zero, arrive Red Line   0   30
distance 750 yards, time 35 yards per minute
Remain 35 minutes
                Leave Red Line at 67, time allowing "A"
and "D" Companies 2 minutes to form up, arrive
Blue Line   100
distance 470 yards, time 15 yards per minute

                9th R. Innis. Fus. arrive Blue line at   3   34
                                   leave   at   3   44
followed by our "A" and "D" Companies - see order
No.10

MOPPING UP   The Company 11th R. Irish Rifles attached mop
up all enemy trenches and Communication Trenches West
of Red Line.
"B" and "C" Companies mop up red line in their own area.
Subsequently they follow "A" and "D" Companies and mop
up "B" Company NAP AVENUE, "C" Company NAP RESERVE,
leaving one section each in red line until relieved by
mopping up Company of 10th R. Innis. Fusrs, when they
rejoin their Companies.

                When the 9th R. Innis Fusrs. advance from Blue
Line "A" and "D" Companies will become their moppers
up. "A" Company will mop up OCEAN SWITCH from
Blue line to OCCASION WEST and OCEAN ALLEY.
"D" Company will mop up OCCASION WEST.

NOMENCLATURE   In making reference to times before or after which
operations will commence, the following nomenclature will
be adopted in future
        (a)   Referring to days
                "Z" day is the day on which operations
                take place.
                        One day before "Z"   "Y" day
                        Two days before "Z"   "X" day
                        Three days before "Z"   "W" day
                        Four days before "Z"   "V" day
                        Five days before "Z"   "U" day
                Days before "U" day will be referred to as
                "Z" minus 6, "Z" minus 7, "Z" minus 8, etc.

                        One day after "Z"   "A" day
                        Two days after "Z"   "B" day
                        Three days after "Z"   "C" day
                Days after "C" day will be referred to as
                "Z" plus 4, "Z" plus 5, "Z" plus 6, etc.

        (b)   Referring to hours on "Z" day
                Zero is the exact time at which operations
                will commence, and times will be designated
                in hours and minutes plus or minus from Zero
                even if they encroach on "Y" day.

MAPS   No marked Maps of any description of our own
lines are to be taken by an Officer, N.C.O. or man in
advance of Battalion Headquarters.

DISTINGUISHING Distinguishing Flags to the number of 4 per
FLAGS   Platoon will be carried attached to the rifle by
Battalion.
                It will be impressed on all ranks that the carrying
of these flags is often the only way by which the
position of our troops can be located.
                Our colour is Orange and Green diagonal.

Officers will wear men's equipment (without ammunition) the pouches will be found useful for field glasses, compass, note book, report forms etc.

If the weather is suitable all ranks will be in shirt sleeves, with the coat in the straps of their pack.

The details carried in the pack, pouches etc as ordered.

Officers Commanding Companies will ensure that the waterbottles are filled.

15. COMMUNICATIONS

The Brigade Forward Station will be established at approximately N.30.a.95.95. and all messages will be sent through this station.

The Brigade Intelligence Officer will establish an Observation post near this point.
(i) Runner Relay Post N.29.b.10.47. (Lt. Murphy responsible for this post.)
(ii) N.24.d.75.10 Junction of NAP AVENUE & NAPIER RESERVE 2nd Lt. C.H.McComb responsible for this post.

16. BRIGADE INTELLIGENCE AND FORWARD COMMUNICATION.

The Brigade Intelligence Personnel will consist of the Brigade Intelligence Officer (2nd Lt. Fitzsimon) 1 other Officer and 14 other ranks (observers and scouts). It will move in rear of our Battalion and endeavour to establish an observation post at N.30.a.80.90. (N.E. of Peckham) in the vicinity of the Brigade Forward Signal Station, which will be at N.30.a.95.95. approximately.

17. BATTALION INTELLIGENCE.

Lt. W.A.Murphy and the Battalion Scouts will form the Intelligence Personnel, their duties are laid down in 36th Div. No. G.S. 2/23 dated 19th inst; and 36th Div. No. G.S. 2/23 dated 25th inst.

The Intelligence Officer will form an observation post in our lines prior to Zero hour. This observation post will remain in use until the next forward one is established, and will also form a relay runner post at N.29.b.10.47.

The Intelligence Officer will arrange for scouts to follow in rear of the assaulting column, but not to take part in the assault.

After capture of Red Line the post will be pushed on to about N.24.d.75.10 and will remain here even after capture of Blue Line, but will send out scouts to keep the C.O. informed as to position of each Unit of the Battalion and such other information as should prove useful.

With reference to Para. 11 of previously quoted letter of the 25th inst, two telescopic rifles will be withdrawn by the Intelligence Officer prior to Zero day, and will be sent into the Quartermaster's stores. The Quartermaster will be responsible for their safe custody.

18. BATTALION ETC INTERCOMMUNICATION

O.C. Company's and Platoon's will take special precautions for keeping touch with the Companies and Platoons respectively on their Right and Left. One of the chief duties of the Company Scouts and Runners is to know where the Companies and Platoons on the Right and Left are, and inform the Company or Platoon Commander the moment they are out of touch, otherwise there is grave danger of having an unguarded flank.

19. SIGNALLING ARRANGEMENTS

2nd Lt. C.H.McComb and the Signallers will keep up the Battalion Inter communication and communication to Brigade. They will follow up the attack, and establish a Battalion Forward post in the Enemy front line in the vicinity of N.30.a.95.95. (Brigade Forward Post). When Blue Line is taken, Battalion Forward Post will be advanced to about N.24.d.76.00. The Brigade Visual Station will be established at the Brigade Forward Station. Divisional Forward Station will be at N.24.c.2.7.

11TH ROYAL INNISKILLING FUSILIERS.

WAR DAIRY

for

MONTH of JULY, 1917.

Army Form C. 2118.

WAR DIARY
or
INTELLIGENCE SUMMARY

11A (S) Batt. Royal Enniskilling Fusiliers

July 1917

(Erase heading not required.)

Place	Date	Hour	Summary of Events and Information	Remarks and references to Appendices
ROUGE CROIX	1/7/17		Map reference HAZEBROUCK 5a. and BELGIUM and FRANCE {1/40,000 SE 1/40,000 CALAIS 13. 1/100,000} Divine Service. Capt. J.S. Hughes, M.C. Struck off the establishment of	
STRAZEELE	2/7/17		Commanding Officers parade at 10.15 a.m. Companies at the disposal of O.C. Companies in the afternoon.	
"	3/7/17		Battalion General inspected the Battalion at 11.0 a.m. afternoon Battn.	
"	4/7/17		O.C. Companies in the morning. Companies at disposal of O.C. Companies and 2.30 p.m. Lecture by Commanding Officer to all Officers and effective N.C.O.'s	
"	5/7/17		Battalion left ROUGE CROIX, STRAZEELE and marched to HONDEGHEM Sub. Area arriving there at 11.0 a.m. in the afternoon Battalion left HONDEGHEM area at 5.0 a.m. for ARQUES arriving	
HONDEGHEM	6/7/17		there at 11.20 a.m. Battalion halted and rest in the afternoon	
ARQUES	7/7/17		Battalion left ARQUES and marched to ARQUINES (distance 16½ miles) arriving there at 11.5 a.m. 2nd Lt. W.H. Clements joined for duty. Divine Service. Companies at the disposal of O.C. Companies	
ARQUINES	8/7/17		for inspection and general refitting.	
"	9/7/17		Training. Notification received that the undermentioned have been awarded the MILITARY MEDAL. 8893 Sgt. Grewes J. 14481 Sgt. Parks J. 14895 L/Cpl. Timm W. 16821 Pte. Beatty J.R. 18315 Sgt. Gardiner W. 14058 Cpl. Edwards J. 9. R17245 L/Cpl McClintock T. 12174 Sgt Hogg S. 29097. Pte Meeke J. (att. 109d. T.M Battery) 29980 Pte Tee Shee P.	

Army Form C. 2118.

July 1917
11th (S) Batt. R. Innishilling Fusiliers.

WAR DIARY
INTELLIGENCE SUMMARY
(Erase heading not required.)

Place	Date	Hour	Summary of Events and Information	Remarks and references to Appendices
ARQUINES	10/7/17		Staff of 21 arrived from Base. Training. Commanding Officer's Kit inspection of "C" and "D" Companies.	
"	11/7/17		Training - Chiefly musketry and Rifle Grenadier. Gas Helmet inspection by Divisional Gas Officer in afternoon.	
"	14/7/17		Battalion Sports at 1 p.m. the field operations was attended, among many representatives of the A.S.C. at the conclusion of the proceedings Lieut-Col. A.C. Pratt D.S.O. presented the prizes.	

RESULTS

TENT PITCHING
1st Sgt Bartlett & Pte Lowry
2nd L/Cpl Agnew and Pte Trillo

BAND RACE
1st Pte McGarvey
2nd C.S.M. Hunter

BICYCLE RACE
1st Pte Wilson
2nd " Clark (A.S.C.)

WRESTLING ON MULES
A.S.C. Team.

SADDLE UP RACE
1st Lieut Ross (A.S.C.)
2nd " Irvine.

FLAT RACE 100 YDS
1st Sgt Guerro
2nd L/Cpl Johnston

OBSTACLE RACE
1st L/Cpl McCarthy
2nd Sgt Cherry

FLAT RACE 440 YDS.
1st Sgt Guerro
2nd " Cherry

FLAT RACE MILE.
1st L/Cpl Ashlers
2nd Pte MacFarland

SACK RACE
1st Pte Lowe
2nd " Mulholland

TUG OF WAR.
1st "A" Coy team
2nd " H " headquarters team

HARM RACE
1st "B" Coy team

PILLOW FIGHT
1st Driver Taggart A.S.C.
2nd Pte Clarke

LONG JUMP
1st L/Cpl Johnston
2nd Pte Burns.

RELAY RACE
1st Pte Johnston & Pte Doherty
2nd " Saunders & " Lynch

3 LEGGED RACE.
1st L/Cpl Johnston & Sgt Agnew
2nd Dr. McKee & Pte. McBurney

SM [signature]

WAR DIARY
11th (S) Batt. R. Enniskilling Fusiliers
INTELLIGENCE SUMMARY

Army Form C. 2118.
July 1917.

Place	Date	Hour	Summary of Events and Information	Remarks and references to Appendices
AQUINES	13/7/17		Training - Brigade Operations.	
"	14/7/17		Training and recreational training.	
"	15/7/17		Divine Service. Brigade Church Parade C.J.E. and Reo. combined at 11.20 a.m. Upon church parade the G.O.C. 36th Division presented the following with the ribbon of their Military Medal:- No. 8893 a/C.S.M. Graves J. "Military Medal" 14451 Sgt- Park J " " 18315 Sgt. Gardiner W.P " " 28980 Pte. McGhee P " " 16821 " Beatty C.R. " " Draft of 4 other ranks arrived from Base. Notification received that Capt. J.M. Forde M.C. has been awarded the Military Cross. "Bar" to Military Cross, and Capt. W.M. Knight "Military Cross" for gallantry during the attack on the WYTSCHAETE - MESSINES Ridge on the 7th June 1917.	
"	16/7/17		Training and Recreational Training including night Operations.	
"	17/7/17		Training and Recreational Training.	
"	18/7/17		Training & Field Exercise. Protection on the line of march and attack on a Position. Recreational Training.	
"	19/7/17		Draft of 11 arrived from Base. Training & Recreational Training.	

Army Form C. 2118.

July 1917.
WAR DIARY
11th (S) Batt. R. Inniskilling Fusiliers
INTELLIGENCE SUMMARY
(Erase heading not required.)

Instructions regarding War Diaries and Intelligence Summaries are contained in F. S. Regs., Part II. and the Staff Manual respectively. Title Pages will be prepared in manuscript.

Place	Date	Hour	Summary of Events and Information	Remarks and references to Appendices
ARQUINES	20/7/17		Training including attack on a Position (Trench Warfare) Notification received 28728 L/Cpl Rutledge has been awarded the "MILITARY MEDAL". Capt L.J. Moir R.A.M.C. joined for duty.	
"	21/7/17		Musketry meeting and Recreational Training.	
"	22/7/17		Divine Service. Battalion met the 14th R.I. Rifles in the Final of the football match for the Brigade Cup Result:- 14th R.I.R. 1 goal 11th R. Innis. Fus. 0	
"	23/7/17		Field Firing exercise. Capt. D.E. Cookie transferred to 110th Lt. Infct.	
"	24/7/17		Field Ambulance for duty. Field Firing exercise.	
"	25/7/17		Battalion drill and Preliminary Battle formations, owing to heavy showers the Battalion had to return. Notification received for Battalion to move to WINNEZEELE area	
"	26/7/17		Battalion moved to WINNEZEELE area (I.N.a.) leaving ARQUINES at 11.45 a.m. and marched to BOISDINGHEM – QUERCAMP and entrained arriving at destination at 7 p.m. Capt. W. Moore and Capt. H.C. Gorton joined.	
WINNEZEELE	29/7/17		Refitting and Training.	
"	28/7/17		Battalion took part in a Brigade Field Exercise and were inspected by Genrl. Sir Hubert Gough Commanding the Fifth Army.	
"	29/7/17		Eight of 72 other ranks arrive from Base. Divine Service. Commanding Officer inspected the Staff.	

Army Form C. 2118.

July 1917
WAR DIARY
11th. (S) Bat. R. Inniskilling Fusiliers
INTELLIGENCE SUMMARY
(Erase heading not required.)

Place	Date	Hour	Summary of Events and Information	Remarks and references to Appendices
WINNEZEELE	30/7/17		Brigadier General of the 109 Brigade inspected the draft. Battalion marched to WATOU area 2.0.11. 4.16.a.9.4. arriving at 12.45.a.m. (midnight) and were accomodated in tents.	
WATOU AREA	31/7/17		Companies at the disposal of O.C. Companies. Awaiting orders for offensive. Weather very dull. Showers at intervals.	

Strength of Battalion 35 Officers 890 other Ranks.

W.C. Pratt. Lieut-Col.
Comdg. 11th. S. Bn. R. Inniskilling Fusiliers.

In the Field
1st August 1917.

CONFIDENTIAL.

ORIGINAL.

WAR DIARY

OF THE

11th (S) BATTALION ROYAL INNISKILLING FUSILIERS.

From 1st August, 1917   To 31st August, 1917

(VOLUME XXIII)

CONFIDENTIAL.

WAR DIARY

11th ROYAL INNISKILLING FUSILIERS.

For Month of AUGUST 1917.

TO, Headquarters,
   109th Inf. Brigade.

   Herewith War Diary of the Battalion under my Command
for Month ending 31st August, 1917.

                                              Lieut-Col.
             Commanding 11th (S) Battn. R. Inniskilling Fus.

IN THE FIELD,
   1st September 1917.

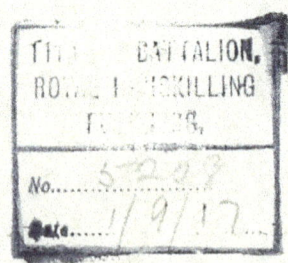

Army Form C. 2118.

WAR DIARY of 11th (S) Battn Royal Innis killing Fusiliers

August 1917

INTELLIGENCE SUMMARY.

(Erase heading not required.)

Instructions regarding War Diaries and Intelligence Summaries are contained in F. S. Regs., Part II. and the Staff Manual respectively. Title pages will be prepared in manuscript.

Place	Date	Hour	Summary of Events and Information	Remarks and references to Appendices
			Map References:- Belgium & France, Sheet 24. Lens 1/100000, France Sheet 56.C.	
WATOU	1:8:17		Strength of Battalion 34 Officers, 881. Other Ranks.	Orders for attack
			Training - Notification received for Battalion to be ready to move off at 2 hours notice. - Artillery Bombardment still progressing -	2 maps showing plan of operations
	2:8:17		Training - Notification received that to move off in 2 hours is cancelled owing to wet weather - Draft of N.C.O.Ks. arrived from Base.	
	3:8:17		Battalion moved to WIELTJE area, and on arrival came under the Command of G.O.C. 10½ Infantry Brigade for tactical purposes. The 10½ Inf. Brigade was holding Front and Support lines (Black and Blue lines). Battalion occupied the lines north side of SAINT JEAN - WIELTJE ROAD - Transport and Quartermasters Stores moved to 1 mile east of POPPERINGHE - Divine Service at 2 p.m. one hour prior to moving off.	
WIELTJE	4:8:17		Situation normal. Trenches in a bad condition owing to wet weather. 1. O.R. wounded -	
	5:8:17		Battalion moved back to VLAMERTINGHE area and were accommodated in	

Army Form C. 2118.

WAR DIARY — 9th (S) Battn. Royal Inniskilling Fusiliers
INTELLIGENCE SUMMARY.

August 1917.

(Erase heading not required.)

Place	Date	Hour	Summary of Events and Information	Remarks and references to Appendices
VLAMERTINGHE	6:8:17		Tents and Bivouacs.	
	7:8:17		Training. The following Officers joined for duty:- 2nd Lieut. J. Finney, 2nd Lieut. J. Malon, 2nd Lieut. S.V. Butler, 2nd Lieut. J.J. Fox, 2nd Lieut. R.J. Barrowman, 2nd Lieut. N. Taylor, 2nd Lieut. J.L. Elsmore, 2nd Lieut. A.H. McCullagh. — taken on strength and establishment of 109 Trench Mortar Battery.	
	8:8:17		Training. T.O.R. joined from Base.	
	9:8:17		Training. Working Parties and Bathing. — Temp. Lieut. W.H. Magenbreiter 23.2.17. Promoted Temp. Captain. 2nd Lieut. E.M. Wilkinson promoted Temp. Lieutenant. 23.2.17. Temp. 2nd Lieut. R.O. Dream, M.C. promoted Temp. Lieutenant. 23.2.17.	
	10:8:17		Training and Working Parties.	
	11:8:17		Working Parties.	
	12:8:17		Working Parties — Divine Service.	
	13:8:17		Training.	
	14:8:17		"X" day. Commanding Officers Parade — Battalion moved to assembly trenches east of WIELTJE in order to take part in the Offensive. "B" and "C" Companies taking over	

WAR DIARY
of 11th (S) Battn. Royal Inniskilling Fusiliers
INTELLIGENCE SUMMARY.

August 1917.

Place	Date	Hour	Summary of Events and Information	Remarks and references to Appendices
			and old Front Line (DURHAM and ADMIRAL Trenches) relieving 8th R.IRISH RIFLES. "A" Company to front line right Company, "D" Company to front line left Company, Left Sub-sector. Headquarters and Carrying Parties to BILGE trench. Heavy bombardment.	
	15:8:17		Situation normal. Casualties 1 O.R. killed 6 O.R. wounded. Bombardment increasing.	
	16:8:17	About 12.30.a.m.	The Commanding Officer was wounded by a shell outside Battalion Headquarters, just as he was about to move to the Assembly Trenches. He died about 15 minutes afterwards - Major J.E.Knott, D.S.O. assumed Command of the Battalion - The Battalion attacked on a four Platoon frontage about 400 yards - "A" Company on the right "D" on the left. "C" Company Left Support, "B" Company right Support. Each Company had two Platoons in leading wave, with one Platoon in support. The 14th Rl. IRISH RIFLES were on the right of the Battalion and the 15th GLOUCESTERS (14½th Brigade) on left. The two leading Companies objective was the GREEN line which they were to mop-up, the rear Companies	

WAR DIARY of 11th (S) Bn. Royal Inniskilling Fusiliers

INTELLIGENCE SUMMARY

August 1917 — Army Form C. 2118.

passing through them to their objective the RED LINE which they were to consolidate by forming certain strong points, for which work Platoons were previously detailed. The Companies detailed to capture GREEN LINE were to follow these Companies and consolidate astred RED LINE. – From GREEN LINE to RED LINE mopping up was to be done by one Platoon each of Support Companies ("A" and "D") – Officer Commanding "A" Company detailed two sections to help right Battalion 14th K.IRISH RIFLES in capture of and to consolidate SCHULER FARM. – Assembly of the Supporting Companies was carried out without serious interference. Heavy shelling was experienced from 1.a.m. to 2.30.a.m. by the left front Company. All the Battalion Headquarters Signallers Apparatus, less a Lucas Lamp, was destroyed by shell fire before ZERO. Barrage commenced at ZERO 4.45 p.m. and on lifting, Companies at once advanced in good order, but were inevitably interfered with by the state of the ground. – The right front Company was met by Machine Gun fire from their left front presumably CASERNE and was considerably reduced. An Officer and 8 men managed to reach 13.A.30.35. but were finally held up by heavy Machine Gun fire from D 13.a.60.75. (see attached map). A messenger sent back giving

WAR DIARY
of 11th (S) Bn. Royal Inniskilling Fusiliers
INTELLIGENCE SUMMARY

(Erase heading not required.)

Army Form C. 2118.

Instructions regarding War Diaries and Intelligence Summaries are contained in F.S. Regs., Part II. and the Staff Manual respectively. Title pages will be prepared in manuscript.

Place	Date	Hour	Summary of Events and Information	Remarks and references to Appendices
			their position was killed and as this party were in the air, and unable to move, they retired at night. Some uncut wire was encountered 50 yards N of CORN HILL which caused some delay. The right supporting Company encountered the same obstacle as the front Company, and by this time were under fire from both POND FARM and CASERNE, JEW HILL and WINNIPEG. This Company was finally held up on a line C.18.f.37. to C.18.f.64. Subsequently connection was made with the left, and this Company assisted in consolidation of FORT HILL which commands all ground to a good all round field of fire. The left front Company "D" encountered severe opposition from FORT HILL (CASERNE) and were held up for some time until they finally stormed it. By this time however our barrage was 1,500 yards away from our troops. While "D" Company were thus engaged, the left support Company endeavoured to push on. Some of their men however became involved in the attack on CASERNE and the remainder, under the Company Commander, having reached N.6.d.2.53. were finally held up by enfilade fire from POND FARM. 20 strong. The Company Commander was then killed, and a few of the survivors crawled back	

WAR DIARY of 9th (S) Bn. Royal Inniskilling Fusiliers
INTELLIGENCE SUMMARY.

Army Form C. 2118.

(Erase heading not required.)

Place	Date	Hour	Summary of Events and Information	Remarks and references to Appendices
			Captain L. J. Moir (R.A.M.C.) wounded Lieut H. J. Dean M.C. wounded	
			2nd Lieut J.D.H. Harrison do 2nd Lieut J.A. Baillie do	
			" " J.J. Kennedy do " " J.C. Sweeny do	
			" " P.W. Johnston do	
			" " W.H. Clements wounded believed missing	
	17:8:17		Battalion moved to VLAMERTINGHE area, and was accommodated in Tents and Bivouacs - Orders received to move that afternoon to WINNIZEELE	
WINNIZELLE VLAMERTINGHE	18:8:17		area at 6 p.m. by Motor Lorries.	
	19:8:17		Roll Call and refitting.	
			Combined Brigade Divine Service - Kit Inspection in afternoon.	
	20:8:17		Training and Medical Inspection - Draft of 35 O.R. arrived from Base	
	21:8:17		Commanding Officer's Parade - Inspection of Kits of Casualties.	
	22:8:17		Routine work.	
	23:8:17		Battalion moved to CAESTRE leaving Camp at 9.45 p.m. entrained and left at 4 a.m. 24th inst detrained at BAPAUME and marched to BARASTRE area and camped about 1 mile north of Town.	

WAR DIARY of 11th (S) Bn. Royal Inniskilling Fusiliers
INTELLIGENCE SUMMARY.

August 1917

Army Form C. 2118.

Place	Date	Hour	Summary of Events and Information	Remarks and references to Appendices
BARASTRE	25.8.17		Refitting and bathing	
	26.8.17		Divine Service - Draft of 114 O.R. arrived from Base.	
	27.8.17		Routine Work.	
	28.8.17		Battalion moved from BARASTRE to NEUVILLE	
NEUVILLE	29.8.17		Battalion moved from NEUVILLE and relieved the 12th Royal Scots in left Sector of Line - Casualties nil -	
	30.8.17		Situation normal - Draft of 9 O.R. arrived from Base.	
	31.8.17		Situation normal. Strength of Battalion 29 Officers, 642 Other Ranks.	
			See attached Orders for Attack, etc.	

Lieut-Col
Commanding 11th (S) Bn. Rl. Inniskilling Fus.

WAR DIARY
of F. M¹. (S) Bn. Royal Inniskilling Fusiliers
INTELLIGENCE SUMMARY

Army Form C. 2118.

(Erase heading not required.)

Place	Date	Hour	Summary of Events and Information	Remarks and references to Appendices

The causes of the holding up were briefly that:- The state of the ground, even had little opposition been met with, prevented the Infantry keeping up with the attack barrage. The enemy machine gun emplacements being intact. Owing the barrage was insufficient to seriously interfere with enemy fire. Owing to the time necessary to storm strong points the barrage was then too far away to provide any protection for the further advance of the troops. The strong points could not be simply passed or left to the mopppers-up, a battle had to be fought for their possession.

The enemy artillery barrage did not interfere with the advance. But the enemy barrage the valley of STEENBEEK in the casualties:-

	Officers	O.Rs.
Killed	4	40
Wounded	6	171
Missing	1	41
Missing believed wounded		4

Black line therefrom the diary and follows

Aug 16/17 APPENDIX 17

Lieut-Col. A.C. PRATT D.S.O killed. 2nd Lieut W. M⁰. E.H. Stewart, killed.
2nd Lieut J. Fluke do. " " J. Carlile do.

SECRET.

BATTALION ORDERS
by
LIEUT-COL. A. C. PRATT, D.S.O.
COMMANDING 11th.(S) BATTN. ROYAL INNISKILLING FUSILIERS.
3.8.17.

1. CHANGE OF STATION.
   The Battalion will move to the WIELTJE area, to-day. On arrival they will come under the Command of the G.O.C. 107th. Infantry Brigade for tactical purposes.
   The 107th. Brigade is holding the Front & Support Lines (Black & Blue lines). The 14th. Royal Irish Rifles will occupy approximately the old British Front & Support Lines about WIELTJE and the 11th. Royal Inniskilling Fusiliers Lines West of 14th. Royal Irish Rifles on the north side of the Saint Jean - Wieltje Road, and South of the Corps boundary.
   The 108th. Infantry Brigade will send Guides to the Asylum to guide the Battalion on arrival by train.
   The Brigade Headquarters will be at G.5.c.

2. MOVE.
   The Battalion will entrain at G.4.d.2.c. at 6.p.m. and will arrive at the entraining point at 5.15.p.m.
   Parade in Full Marching Order ready to move off at 3.15.p.m.
   The Transport will be located at G.5.c.

3. CAMP.
   The Camp will be left thoroughly clean and will be handed over by the Adjutant to the Temporary Camp Warden. Number of tents 71. Receipt to be obtained for tents handed over. Temporary Camp Warden will be instructed to take receipt for tents when handing over to relieving Unit.

4. BILLETING PARTIES.
   Billeting Parties for Battalion will report to Staff Captain at WIELTJE at 11.30.a.m. and representatives of the Transport will meet Assistant Staff Captain at G.5.c. at 10.a.m to take over Transport Lines and representatives of the Transport will meet Brigade Transport Officer at H.8.a.7.2. at 11.a.m.
   Quartermaster's Stores and Transport Billets for night 3/4th August will be as follows:- Personnel C.27.c. Stores and Transport G.5.c. Billets for the 4th & 5th and until further orders, Personnel do not move, Stores & Transport H.8.a.7.2.
   Extra Transport Baggage Waggons at present with Units will remain with them until further orders.

5. BILLETING CERTIFICATES.
   Billeting Officer will prepare and submit to area Commandant before leaving the WATOU area, Billeting Certificates.

6. SANITATION.
   On arrival in new area the usual Sanitary arrangements will be made.

7. SUPPLY.
   Rations will be delivered by train at Transport Lines of Units for consumption the following day.

8. FIELD POST OFFICE.
   The 109th. Brigade Field Post Office will move to Brigade Transport Lines at H.8.a.7.2. on 3rd.inst.

9. ORDNANCE.
   Ordnance will be drawn from Divisional H.Q. commencing 4th.inst.

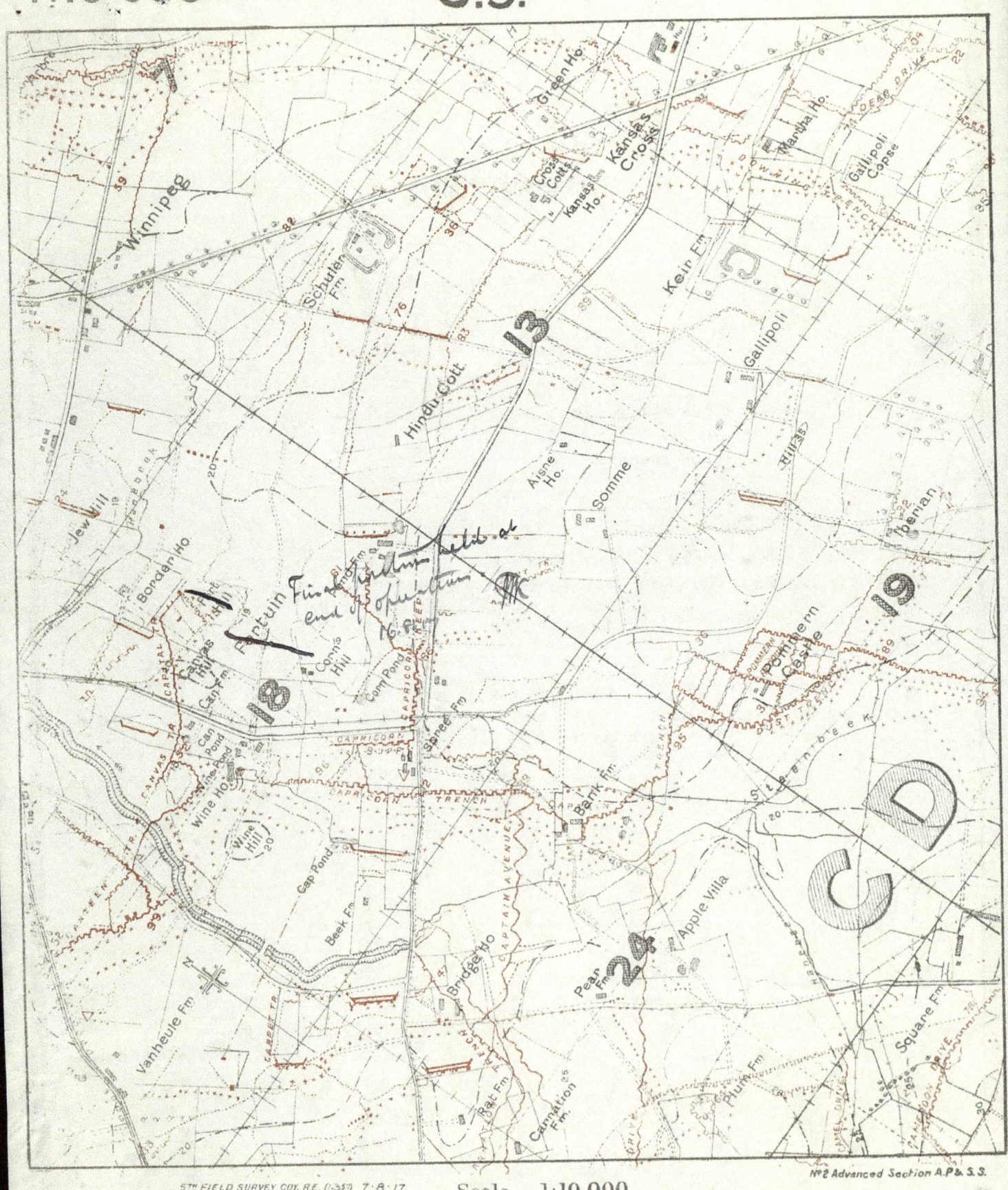

Message Form.

..............Division.

Map reference or mark own position on Map at back.

I am at..

I am at..and am consolidating.

I am at..and have consolidated.

I need :—Ammunition.
      Bombs.
      Rifle Grenades.
      Water.
      Very lights.
      Stokes shells.

Enemy forming up for counter attack at..

I am in touch with......................on Right / Left at........................

I am not in touch on Right. / Left.

Am being shelled from..

I estimate my present strength at................rifles.

Hostile (Battery / Machine Gun / Trench Mortar) active at..........................

Time   a.m. (p.m.)   Name................................

Date..............................   Platoon............ Company............

Place...............................   Battalion................................

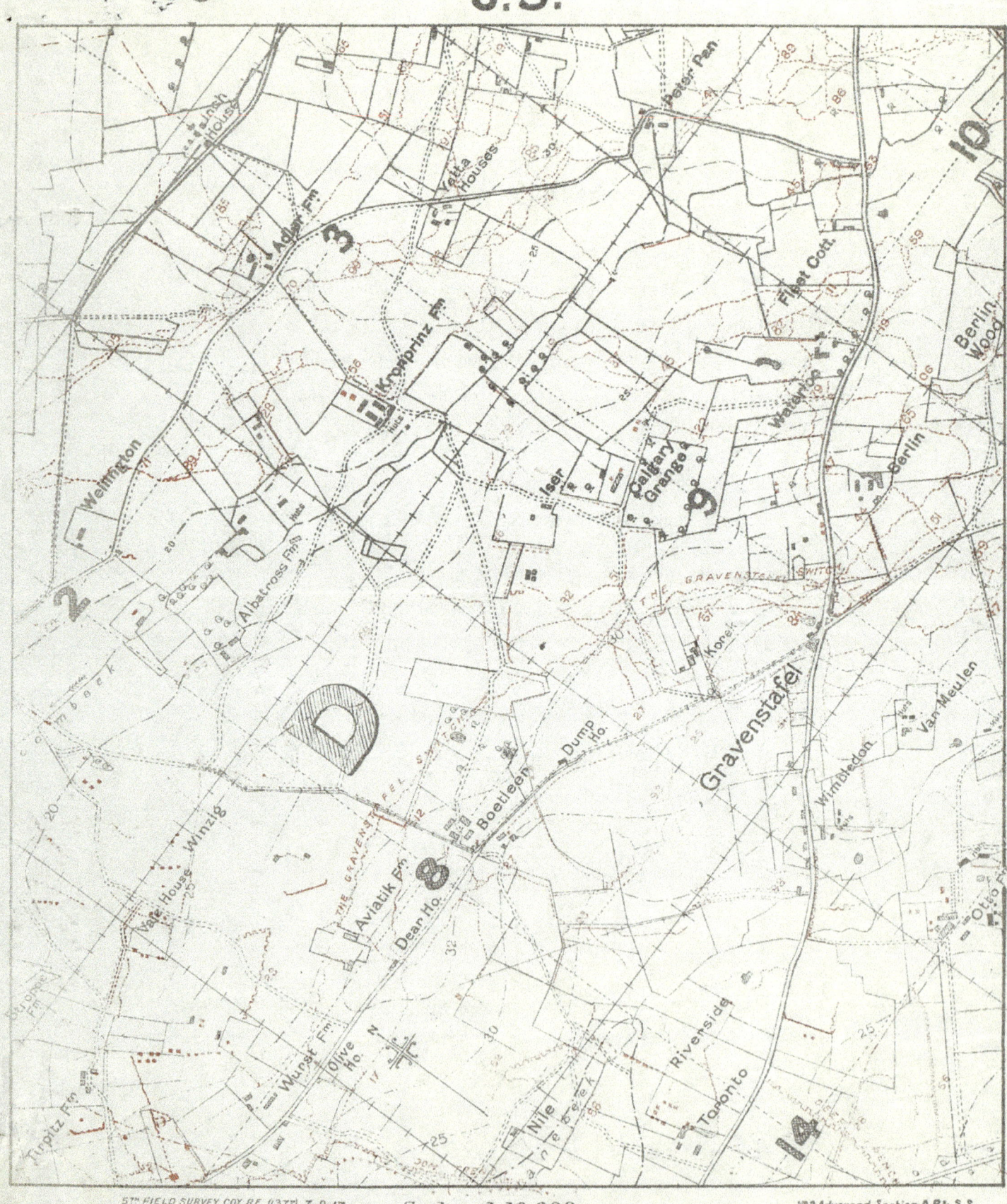

Message Form.

..............Division.

Map reference or mark own position on Map at back.

I am at..

I am at..and am consolidating.

I am at..and have consolidated.

I need :—Ammunition.
       Bombs.
       Rifle Grenades.
       Water.
       Very lights.
       Stokes shells.

Enemy forming up for counter-attack at............................

I am in touch with....................on Right / Left at....................

I am not in touch on Right. / Left.

Am being shelled from............................

I estimate my present strength at..............rifles.

Hostile { Battery / Machine Gun / Trench Mortar } active at............................

Time   a.m. (p.m.)   Name............................

Date............................   Platoon............ Company............

Place............................   Battalion............................

SECRET   Copy, No. 2

INSTRUCTIONS FOR THE OFFENSIVE
by
LIEUT-COL. A. C. PRATT, D.S.O.
COMMANDING 11th (S) Battn. Royal Inniskilling Fusiliers.

13:8:17.

IN CONTINUATION OF OPERATION ORDERS of 1:8:17.

ORDER, No. 3.   Add "No marked Maps of our lines are to be taken by any Officer, or N.C.O. or man beyond Battalion H.Q."

ORDER, No. 4.   Cancelled, and the following substituted. " S.O.S. Signal, Green Lights fired from Very Pistols to be continued until Artillery barrage commences, but a change may be ordered at any time to the Rifle Grenade Rocket, therefore it is requisite to have them in addition"

ORDER, No. 8.   Flag will be a white Signaller's flag with Castle of Inniskilling in blue, XI below it, and a blue border.

ORDER, No. 11.   Rifleman 200 rounds S.A.A., instead of 170 rounds and the 2 No. 5 Bombs.
Every Bombing Section and every Mopping up Squad will carry 4 MSK Grenades filled with KJ or, if these are not available, P. Grenades.

ORDER, No. 24.   ADD "The Regimental Sergeant Major will take charge of Prisoners captured by the Battalion, they will be handed over to him from Company escorts at about C.18.c.8.8. (Black Line). He will pass them on to SPREE FARM (C.18.d.1.3) Prisoners will be used to bring back our casualties and salvage".

ORDER, No. 28.   Watson Fans will be carried, one by one of the Company H.Q. Signallers and two by each Platoon, they are used by front line troops.
No. 21 Squadron R.F.C. will detail a Contact Patrol Aeroplane to work with Attacking Divisions during the attack.

Flares will be lit by the Infantry in the front line, and Watson Fans waved:-
(a) When called upon to do so by the Contact Aeroplane by means of Klaxon Horns and Very Lights.
This call will, if the attack proceeds as arranged, only to be made at times when the Infantry are believed to have reached the Green Line and the final Objective.
(b) When the Infantry consider it advisable to make known the position of their front line.

RED FLARES will be used.
Contact Aeroplanes will be marked with a BLACK PLAQUE projecting behind the right lower wing.
In addition to the above Contact Aeroplane, one Infantry Protection Machine will be in the air from ZERO hour until dark. This Machine will carry no distinctive marking.
40 Watson Fans will be issued to each Battalion.

ORDER, No. 29.   Does not now apply.

1. ATTACK: The Battalion will attack on a date and at a time to be notified later, with the 14th Batt. R.IRISH RIFLES on the Right, the 1st/5th GLOUCESTER Regiment (48th Division) on the left.

The 9th Battn. R.INNIS. FUS. will be in support and the 10th Battn. R. INNIS. FUS. in Brigade Reserve.

32. DISPOSITION FOR ATTACK "A" and "D" Companies lead the attack, with "A" Company on the right and "D" Company on the left, supported at 250 yards distance by "B" and "C" Companies respectively.

"A" and "D" Companies will each have 2 Platoons in the first wave and its third Platoon in the second wave.
Similarly "B" and "C" Companies will be in 2 waves.
Each wave will be in 2 lines at 25 to 50 yards distance.
Each Company has a front of about 225 yards.
The magnetic bearing of the line of Attack is roughly 65 degrees.

33. ASSEMBLY. Companies will be placed as follows:-
On X Y night "A" and "D" Companies will take over Black Line north of C.18.c.90.95. from 107th Brigade.
"B" and "C" Companies will be in support in our old front line trenches (DURHAM ARMITAGE ADMIRAL) north of WIELTJE road and South of Corps Boundary.
Behind them will be the 9th. R.INNIS.FUS. in BILGE trench and GARDEN STREET and in rear of them 10th R.INNIS. FUS. in LIVERPOOL TRENCH.
Battalion H.Q. will be WIELTJE Mine-shaft.
Troops proceed in position by No. 6. track.
"A" and "D" Companies as they pass the Battalion Dump situated at C.22.d.6.2. will pick up their battle stores, such as Bombs, Rifle Grenades, Water etc.
On Y.Z. night "B" and "C" Companies having collected from the dump during the day their battle stores, will proceed so as to be in position in rear of "A" and "D" Companies respectively, prior to zero hour.

No. 34. BOUNDARIES. Right boundary junction of trench C.18.c.88.60. C.18.b.08.63. SCHULER FARM (exclusive, but to be eventually garrisoned by us vide Order No. 36) D.7.d.85.40. - D.8.c.75.70.
Left boundary, point where CANTEEN TRENCH crosses the STEENBEEK - BORDER HOUSE (exclusive) road junction D.7.c.26.54. Hedge Corner D.7.b.85.28.
Dividing line between Companies.
C.18.c.70.90.   D.13.a.00.80.
D.7.d.00.40.   D.8.a.00.05.
D.8.a.70.50.

No. 35. ATTACK. "A" & "D" Companies will assault Green Line, & will each have 2 Sections of 9th R.INNIS FUS. to Mop-up for them. As these Sections will probably be very weak they will be returned to O.C. 9th R.INNIS.FUS. after consolidation of Green Line. Each Mopping-up Squad will carry 4 MSK or P Grenades in addition to ordinary equipment.
The Artillery barrage will halt for 20 minutes beyond Green Line when "B" and "C" Companies will close up and when the barrage lifts will pass through to the Attack on red line. "A" and "D" Companies following in close support - the Green Line being taken over by the 9th R.INNIS.FUS.
"A" and "D" Companies will each supply one Platoon to mop up for "B" & "C" Companies respectively.
In addition O.C. "A" Company will supply 2 Sections to assist in attack on SCHULER FARM. They will then turn it, or if preferable, the trench in its vicinity, into a strong point and will garrison it. Each man of these two sections will carry 4 MSK bombs filled with KJ or P Grenades, if the former are not available.

No. 36.
OBJECTIVE.

The final objective is the portion of the CHELUVELT - LANGEMARCK line between our forward boundaries. The forward line however to be consolidated will be in advance of this line and will include AVIATIK FARM.

No. 37.
MAP OF BOUNDARIES and OBJECTIVES.

(a) The right and left boundaries of the Brigade (in YELLOW)
(b) The intermediate line (in GREEN).
(c) The approximate line to be consolidated by the Supporting Battalions (in DOTTED GREEN).
(d) The final objective (in DOTTED RED).
(e) The forward line to be consolidated (in SOLID RED).
(f) The dividing line between attacking Battalions (in BLUE)

IN MARKING REPORTS OFFICERS WILL BE CAREFUL TO USE THE NEW COLOUR NAMES FOR THE VARIOUS LINES.

No. 38.
CONSOLIDATION.

On arrival at the final objective, 2 lines will be consolidated, the forward line being that marked in RED and the back line being that marked as a DOTTED RED LINE.

The points in these lines which will be the first to be consolidated are those ringed round with a red line. Definite Platoons must be told off for the capture of these points and these Platoons will at once consolidate them.

A half section of an R.E. Field Company will be allotted to the Battalion to provide technical assistance in the consolidation of these forward points. They will be attached to "B" and "C" Companies equally.

The DOTTED RED LINE will be consolidated by the rear Companies of the Assaulting Battalions.

9th. R. INNIS. FUS. (Support Battalion) will move forward from the GREEN LINE as soon as the final objective has been taken and will consolidate the approximate line marked in DOTTED GREEN on Map "A".

It must be understood that no attempt can be made in the first case to consolidate a continuous line in the above positions. Efforts will be concentrated on the enemy strong points which have not been demolished by our artillery and on portions of trenches or sections of ground which are of tactical value for providing cross fire over the intervening spaces.

Traverses to be erected to screen from right front in particular.

Portable entrenching tools will not be carried. 50% of each Company will carry full size entrenching tools. The proportion of picks to shovels will be 1 to 5.

No. 39.
TANKS.

1 Section "F" Battn. 3rd. Bde. Tanks Corps, is allotted to the Division. The weather conditions make it very uncertain whether the tanks can be employed at all, and in any case they cannot get up in time to keep up with the Infantry in the Attack.

If they can be employed at all, they will therefore assist in "mopping up" isolated points which still continue to hold out.

No. 40.
BATTALION H.Q.

Battalion H.Q. on YZ night from Zero minus 1 hour will be about C.18.c.8.9.

On capture of GREEN LINE to C.18.a.2.6. Caserne S.E. of BORDER HOUSE.

On capture of final objective to about D.7.d.

No. 41. PACK. The Pack will contain the following:-
Emergency Ration, Two days' rations, Ground Sheet, 1 pair socks, 1 Bandolier, Lemon (if issued) Candle, Matches, etc.
Shovel will be carried outside the Pack.

No. 42. ANTI-AIRCRAFT. When occupying a trench line or during consolidation, 1 section of each Platoon will be on duty to deal with low flying enemy air-craft - one man of the section to be on sentry, the remainder to have their rifles ready.

No. 43. SCOUTS. The Battalion Intelligence Officer will detail :-
(a) 1 Scout to be at disposal of each O.C. Company.
(B) to liason with Battalions on right and left and keep him informed as to the progress of these Battalions.
(c) Two Scouts to be attached to carrying parties.
(d) Two Snipers to "B" Company and two to "C" Company to observe and act as Snipers during and after consolidation.

No. 44. INFORMATION & COMMUNICATION. O.C. Companies and Scouts have been issued with Post Card Maps.
Reports to be sent by Runners and messages by Runners or Visual Signal.
There will be a Brigade Runner relay post at SPREE FARM and a forward one will be established at POND FARM. After capture of final objective, a runner relay post and Brigade Signal Station will be at SCHULER FARM.

(Sgd)   H.C. GORDON.   Captain.

A/Adjutant, 11th (S) Bn. R. Inniskilling Fus.

COPIES TO:-
1. 109th. Brigade.
2. Commanding Officer.
3. Adjutant.
4. O.C. "A" Coy.
5. O.C. "B" "
6. O.C. "C" "
7. O.C. "D" "
8. O.C. Details, Quartermaster & Transport Officer.
9. Intelligence Officer.
10. 9th. R. Innis. Fus.
11. 10th. R. Innis. Fus.
12. 14th. R. Irish Rifles.
13. 109th. M.G. Coy.
14. 109th. T.M.B.
15. 1/5th. Gloucester Regt.
16. Signal Sergeant.
17. War Diary.

SECRET.

BATTALION ORDERS
by
MAJOR J. E. KNOTT, D.S.O.
COMMANDING 11th (S) BATTN. ROYAL INNISKILLING FUSILIERS.

28.8.1917

1. The Battalion will relieve the 12th R.SCOTS in LEFT SECTOR, night 29/30th inst. "B" Company RIGHT of Front Line, "C" Company LEFT of Front Line, "A" Company in SUPPORT "D" Company in RESERVE.

2. Company Stores, Officer's Kits etc will be dumped at Orderly Room at 6.p.m. Companies will arrange loading Parties.

3. The Battalion will parade in Main Street at 7.p.m. to entrain at P.22.c.44.
    On arrival of train at HERCUES. Platoons will march off in the following order:- Headquarters "C" Company "B" Company "D" Company "A" Company 100 yards distance between Platoons. NO smoking or lights on the March. Companies will carry their Lewis Guns and ammunition, 24 Magazines per Gun.

4. Guides of 12th R.SCOTS. will be provided as follows, and will meet at WINDY CORNER at 9.p.m.
    "B" & "C" Companies, 1 Guide per post.
    "A" & "D" Companies, 1 Guide per Platoon.
    O.C. 12th R.SCOTS is arranging for each Guide to have a Chit saying for which post he is acting as Guide. Officers Commanding Companies will see that Commander of each Post has a Chit saying to which Post he is going.

5. O.C.Companies will send up an Officer and N.C.O. (O.C.front Companies in addition a representative of their Lewis Gun Teams) to take over Trench Stores and make themselves familiar with the trenches at 11.a.m. at ¼ hour intervals in order "B", "C", "D", "A".
    N.C.O. in charge of Signals will also send a Representative.
    These N.C.Os will not carry their Packs but will hand them over to Company Quarter Master Sergeants to be sent up with Rations. They will report at Headquarters of Battalion in line.

6. Companies on arrival in trenches, will immediately get into touch with Companies on their Flanks.

7. Dress:- Field Service Marching Order. Water Bottle filled.

8. Relief to be wired in Code to Battalion Headquarters.

9. List of Trench Stores, duly countersigned, will be rendered to Orderly Room by 10.a.m. 30/8/17.

10. Companies will submit by 10.a.m. 30/8/17, a Sketch shewing their dispositions
    1. By day
    2. By night.
    Including Company Dumps, Latrines, Bomb & S.A.A. Stores.

(Sgd) W. MOORE Captain & Adjutant
11th (S) Battn. Royal Inniskilling Fusiliers.

Copies to :-
109th Brigade,	O.C. "C" Coy,	Quartermaster,
Commanding Officer,	O.C. "D" Coy,	R.S.M.
Adjutant,	Medical Officer	War Diary,
O.C.12th R.Scots,	Intelligence Officer,	File.
O.C. "A" Coy,	N.C.O. i/c Signals,	
O.C. "B" Coy,	Transport Officer,	

10. **FIELD CASHIER.**

XIXth Corps Field Cashier's Office at School Camp, POPPERINGHE, A.28.d.7.5. will be open every morning from 10. to 12.noon, and every afternoon, except Sunday, 3 to 4.p.m.

11. **DIVINE SERVICE.**

The Battalion Order of last night is amended to 2.p.m.

(Sgd) E.M.Wilkinson. 2nd.Lieut.
A/Adjutant, 11th (S) Battn. Rl. Inniskilling Fuslrs.

COPIES to:-
109th. Inf. Brigade.
Commanding Officer.
O.C. "A" Company.
O.C. "B" "
O.C. "C" "
O.C. "D" "
Intelligence Officer.
Medical Officer.
Transport Officer.
Quartermaster.
Signalling Officer.
R.S.M.
War Diary (2)
File.

CONFIDENTIAL.

WAR DIARY

of

11th BATTALION ROYAL INNISKILLING FUSILIERS

Period   1st September 1917
         to
         30th September 1917.

September 1917. WAR DIARY of 11th (S) Bn Rl. Innis Killing Fusrs

INTELLIGENCE SUMMARY

(Erase heading not required.)

Army Form C. 2118.

Place	Date	Hour	Summary of Events and Information	Remarks and references to Appendices
HERMIES	1st		Map Reference HERMIES 1/10.000. Strength of Battalion 29 Officers and 843 other Ranks. Battalion in trenches HERMIES Sector, Situation normal	
BERTINCOURT SECTOR	2nd		Situation normal	
	3rd		Situation normal	
	4th		Situation normal	
	5th		Situation normal	
BERTINCOURT	6th		Battalion was relieved in the trenches by 9th (S) Bn Rl. Innis Fus, and went back to Brigade Reserve. One Other Rank Killed by shell fire	
	7th		Refitting and Bathing	
	8th		Training, Bathing and Working Parties	
	9th		Working Parties, Divine Service	
	10th		Battalion was inspected by 4th Corps Commander. Working Parties	
	11th		Training and Working Parties	
	12th		Training and Working Parties	

Army Form C. 2118.

WAR DIARY
September 1917, of 11th (S) Bn. Rl. Innis. Fus
INTELLIGENCE SUMMARY.
(Erase heading not required.)

Place	Date	Hour	Summary of Events and Information	Remarks and references to Appendices
HERMIES. LEFT SUB.SECTOR	13th		Battalion relieved 9th (S) Bn. Rl. Innis. Fus. in HERMIES Sector. "A" and "D" Coys in front line, "B" Coy in Support and "C" Coy in Reserve	
	14th		Situation normal.	
	15th		Situation normal. 2nd Lieuts. A.J. Start, P.V.J. Reade, A.H. Patterson W.H. Gurdy joined for duty. Draft of 11 arrived from Base.	
	16th		Situation normal. Companies carried out an inter Company relief	
	17th		Situation normal. "B" and "C" Coys front line, "A" Coy in Support, and "D" Coy in Reserve.	
	18th		Situation normal. The following have been awarded the military medal. 20476 Sgt Warren, J. 8390 Cpl Scott, J. 17308 L/Cpl Elliott, W. 16205 Cpl Johnston, S. 11068 Pte Donnell, S. 43032 Pte Orrill, F. 27869 Pte Ferguson, W.K.	
	19th		Situation normal.	
	20th		Situation normal. The following have been awarded the military Cross. Capt. B. M. F. Stone, 2nd Lieut. T.C. Sweeny, The Rev. A. Spence. One other Rank wounded.	

Army Form C. 2118.

WAR DIARY
of 11th (S) Bn. R.l. Innis. Fusrs.

September 1917.

INTELLIGENCE SUMMARY.

(Erase heading not required.)

Instructions regarding War Diaries and Intelligence Summaries are contained in F. S. Regs., Part II. and the Staff Manual respectively. Title pages will be prepared in manuscript.

Place	Date	Hour	Summary of Events and Information	Remarks and references to Appendices
BERTINCOURT	21st		Battalion was relieved in HERMIES Sector by 9th (S) Bn. R.l. Innis. Fusrs. and went back to Brigade Reserve.	
	22nd		Bathing, Refitting and Medical Inspection.	
	23rd		Divine Service	
	24th		Training and Working Parties.	
	25th		Training and Working Parties.	
	26th		Training and Working Parties.	
	27th		Training and Working Parties.	
	28th		Training and Working Parties. Divl. commander inspected Transport, Transport lines, and Billets. 2nd Lieut. D. Neil joined for duty. 46 other Ranks arrived from Reinforcement Camp.	
HERMIES.	29th		Battalion relieved 9th (S) Bn. R.l. Innis. Fusrs. in HERMIES Sector "B" and "C" Coy's Front line, "A" Coy in Support, "D" Coy in Reserve.	
LEFT SUB. SECTION	30th		Situation Normal. Capt. S. M. Forde M.C. joined for duty. Strength of Battalion 31 Officers and 709 other Ranks.	

McC[?] Lieut-Col
Comdg 11th (S) Bn. R. Innis. Fusrs.

Confidential

TO, 109th Inf. Bde.

      Herewith WAR DIARY of the Battalion under my Command for month ending 31st October, 1917.

                                        Lieut-Col.,
            Commanding 11th (S) Bn. R. Inniskilling Fuslrs.

In the Field,
   31st October, 1917.

CONFIDENTIAL. ORIGINAL.

WAR DIARY

of the

11th (SERVICE) BATTALION ROYAL INNISKILLING FUSILIERS.

From 1st OCTOBER, 1917. TO 31st OCTOBER, 1917.

(VOLUME XXV)

Army Form C. 2118.

WAR DIARY
of 11th (S) Bn. R¹ Inniskilling Fusiliers
INTELLIGENCE SUMMARY.

October, 1917.

(Erase heading not required.)

Instructions regarding War Diaries and Intelligence Summaries are contained in F. S. Regs., Part II. and the Staff Manual respectively. Title pages will be prepared in manuscript.

Place	Date	Hour	Summary of Events and Information	Remarks and references to Appendices
Demicourt	1/10/17	-	Strength: 31 Officers 709 Otherranks. Battalion in the Trenches (HERMIES sector) Situation normal.	
"	2/10/17	-	Situation normal.	
"	3/10/17	-	Situation normal.	
"	4/10/17	-	Situation normal.	
"	5/10/17	-	Situation normal	
"	6/10/17	-	Situation normal	
"	7/10/17	-	Battalion was relieved in the trenches by the 9th (S) Bn R. Inniskilling Fusiliers and went back to Brigade Reserve. Situation Normal.	
Beaumetz	8/10/17		Bathing, Medical Inspection and refitting.	
"	9/10/17		Training and Working Parties. Draft of 16 arrives from Divisional Depot Battⁿ	
"	10/10/17		Training and Working Parties.	
"	11/10/17		Training and Working Parties. The following Officers joined for duty today: 2nd Lieut. W. A. Baker; 2nd Lt. Gurmilnie; 2nd Lt. J. M. Robinson; 2nd Lt. A. H. Buckley; 2nd Lt. H.S. Legg.	
"	"		Draft of 14 arrives from 36th Divisional Depot Battalion	
"	12/10/17		Training and Working Parties	

WAR DIARY of 11th (S) Bn R. Inniskilling Fusiliers

Army Form C. 2118.

October 1917

INTELLIGENCE SUMMARY

(Erase heading not required.)

Place	Date	Hour	Summary of Events and Information	Remarks and references to Appendices
Berincourt	13/10/17		Training and Working Parties	
-"-	14/10/17		Divine Service. Lecture by R.S.M. to all N.C.O.'s	
-"-	15/10/17		Training. Battalion relieved 9th (S) Bn R. Inniskilling Fusiliers in HERMIES	
-"-			Left sub-sector.	
Demicourt	16/10/17		Situation normal.	
-"-	17/10/17		Situation normal.	
-"-	18/10/17		Situation normal.	
-"-	19/10/17		Situation normal.	
-"-	20/10/17		Situation normal.	
-"-	21/10/17		Situation normal. 1 O.R. wounded.	
-"-	22/10/17		Situation normal. 2 Other ranks wounded (Accidently)	
-"-	23/10/17		Battalion was relieved by the 9th Bn Royal Inniskilling Fusiliers in the HERMIES	
-"-	"		Left sub-sector. (See attached Relief Orders)	
Berincourt	24/10/17		Training. Medical Inspection and Bathing. Commanding Officers inspection	
-"-	"		Major D.G. Whittla joined for duty.	
-"-	25/10/17		Training & Working Parties. Draft 20 of 10 joined from Divisional Reinforcement Camp.	
-"-	26/10/17		Training and Working Parties. 2nd Lieuts A.P. Hughes, J.P. Gray and R. Abraham joined for duty.	

Army Form C. 2118.

WAR DIARY
or ~~INTELLIGENCE SUMMARY~~

of 11th (S) Bn R¹ Inniskilling Fusiliers

October 1917

(Erase heading not required.)

Place	Date	Hour	Summary of Events and Information	Remarks and references to Appendices
Berlincourt	27/10/17		Training and Working Parties.	
"	28/10/17		Divine Service	
"	29/10/17		Training and Working Parties.	
"	30/10/17		Training and Working Parties.	
"	31/10/17		Commanding Officer's parade. Battalion relieved 9th Bn Royal Inniskilling Fusiliers in HERMIES left Sub-sector. (see attached Relief Order)	
			Strength of Battalion: 44 Officers. 726 Other Ranks.	

In the Field.
31st October 1917.

[signature]
Lieut-Col.
Comdg. 11th (S) Bn Royal Inniskilling Fusiliers

11th B. Inniskilling Fusiliers.

W A R   D I A R Y

for period from 1st to 30th November, 1917.

CONFIDENTIAL

WAR DIARY

OF THE

11TH (S) BATTALION ROYAL INNISKILLING FUSILIERS

1ST NOVEMBER 1917   TO   30 NOVEMBER 1917.

VOLUME XXVI

Army Form C. 2118.

WAR DIARY INTELLIGENCE SUMMARY

11th (S) Bn. Royal Inniskilling Fusiliers, November, 1917.

(Erase heading not required.)

Instructions regarding War Diaries and Intelligence Summaries are contained in F. S. Regs., Part II. and the Staff Manual respectively. Title pages will be prepared in manuscript.

Place	Date	Hour	Summary of Events and Information	Remarks and references to Appendices
Hermies	1/11/17		Map FRANCE Sheet 57 C NE Ed. 7A 1/20000	
"	"		Strength 44 Officers 725 OR Battalion in trenches Hermies Left Sub Sector. Situation normal	
"	2/11/17		Situation normal.	
"	3/11/17		Situation normal.	
"	4/11/17		Situation normal. 2nd Lieuts J. McClelland. 6 R Kitson. J. D. MacCarthy joined for duty	
"	5/11/17		Situation normal	
"	6/11/17		Situation normal. Battalion was relieved by 9th Battalion Rl Innis Fus and went back to Brigade Reserve	
Bertincourt	7/11/17		Training. Bathing and Medical Inspection	
"	8/11/17		Training and Working Parties	
"	9/11/17		Training and Working Parties	
"	10/11/17		Training and Working Parties	
"	11/11/17		Divine Service and Working Parties	
"	12/11/17		Training. Working Parties and Medical Inspection. Battalion relieved 9th Rl Innis	

WAR DIARY
or
INTELLIGENCE SUMMARY.
(Erase heading not required.)

Army Form C. 2118.

Instructions regarding War Diaries and Intelligence Summaries are contained in F. S. Regs., Part II. and the Staff Manual respectively. Title pages will be prepared in manuscript.

Place	Date	Hour	Summary of Events and Information	Remarks and references to Appendices
Bertincourt	Nov 12th 1917		in Hermies left Sub-Sector (see attached)	Battalion Order No. 76
Hermies	13		Situation Normal.	
"	14		Situation Normal. 2nd Lieut. S.J. Soper. G.E.S. Mitchell. W. Grantham joined for duty	
"	15		Situation Normal. Lieut J.W. Charlton joined for duty	
"	16		Situation Normal. Battalion was relieved by 2 Companies of 14th R. Irish Rifles and went back to Velu Wood, where it was accommodated in tents and bivouacs (see attached)	Battalion Order No. 77
Velu Wood	17		Training and refitting for Offensive. Working Parties	
"	18		Divine Service. Training and Working Parties	
"	19		Refitting for offensive	
"	20		Battalion left Velu Wood to take part in the offensive at 1.0am to the assembly trenches. Assembly was carried out without interruption and equipment was given out to the troops who then rested until ordered to move up to the attack. The Battalion moved up to our front line sustaining a few	Battalion Orders dated 17.11.17 and Order No 78

WAR DIARY
OR
INTELLIGENCE SUMMARY.
(Erase heading not required.)

Army Form C. 2118.

Place	Date	Hour	Summary of Events and Information	Remarks and references to Appendices
Hebuterne	20		casualties on the way. It followed closely on the heels of the 9th Royal Inniskilling Fusiliers. "A" Coy, (Capt. Wm Knight M.C.) plus 1 Platoon of "B" Coy, leading off northwards up "L" Trench and Canal DU NORD, "D" Coy (Lieut R.M. Barrowman) up "B" trench (German support line). "C" Coy, (Capt. W.A. Wagentrieber) up "A" trench (German front line) with 2 Lewis Gun teams of "B" Coy in Battalion Reserve, "B" Coy, less 1 Platoon and 2 Lewis Gun teams acted as Carrying Company. The 9th Royal Inniskilling Fusiliers going on ahead encountered considerable resistance in both "A" and "L" trenches about K 9.a 8.2 and K 8.6 8.0 respectively and were assisted by our Companies coming up. Fights at both places mentioned occurred. "C" Coy, of this Battalion had 4 killed and accounted for 8 of the enemy who were holding them up by bombing and machine gun fire. "A" Company and "D" Company quickly pushed on however and passed the 9th Royal Inniskilling Fusiliers at their objective which was roughly a line K 3.d 2.3 to K 3.c 0.25. "A" and "D" Companies arrived at Lock No 6 at 1.10 P.M. where they were held up by machine gun fire. The 62nd Division on the East side of the Canal were held up from the same place & were behind our men.	

WAR DIARY
INTELLIGENCE SUMMARY.
(Erase heading not required.)

Army Form C. 2118.

Place	Date	Hour	Summary of Events and Information	Remarks and references to Appendices
Enemy's Trenches	20		2nd Lieut. J. Finney went back and arranged with them to send on 2 Tanks which was done and the garrison of Rock 6 then retired over the SPOIL HEAP at E.27.c.5.1. not being fired on by "A" Company's Lewis Guns which inflicted numerous casualties. "A" and "D" Companies then pushed in and obtained their objective about E.26.d.8.7. By about 3.30 P.M. "C" Company had leap-frogged the 9th Royal Inniskilling Fusiliers at their objective and pushed on encountering little resistance in turn they reached their objective at about E.26.d.2.2. at 4.30 P.M. It was nearly dark and the Battalion was immediately reorganised in depth and consolidation commenced "C" and "D" Companies holding the objective with "A" Company on a line 150 yards south of the BAPAUME-CAMBRAI ROAD with Battalion Headquarters in Battalion reserve at K.3.a.5.2. Touch was obtained with 2/5 West Riding Regiment (62nd Division) on our right at E.26.d.9.8 and at about 2 A.M. night of 20/21 November with 56th Division at E.20.I.8 on the left.	
	21		Strong patrols were sent out Northwards up tracks in direction of MOEUVRES one of which encountered opposition and was driven back by Rifle fire at about E.20.c.9.2. Otherwise no opposition was encountered and	

Army Form C. 2118.

WAR DIARY
INTELLIGENCE SUMMARY.
(Erase heading not required.)

Instructions regarding War Diaries and Intelligence Summaries are contained in F. S. Regs., Part II. and the Staff Manual respectively. Title pages will be prepared in manuscript.

Place	Date	Hour	Summary of Events and Information	Remarks and references to Appendices
Enemy's Trenches	21		No counter-attack was experienced during the night 20/21. The 9th Royal Inniskilling Fusiliers, 10th Royal Inniskilling Fusiliers and 14th Royal Irish Rifles passed through our lines towards MOEUVRES early on the morning of 21st November. Casualties - Killed 6 Other Ranks WOUNDED 1 OFFICER and 25 Other Ranks	
"	22		Battalion was relieved by 9th Royal Irish Fusiliers (108th Brigade) who continued the attack and went back to HERMIES where they rested.	
HERMIES.	23		Resting and refitting	
"	24		Battalion left HERMIES and relieved 2 companies of 2nd R.I.R. and 2 companies R.Ir. Fus with Headquarters at E.26.5. in 9.9.	
Enemy's Trenches	25		Battalion was relieved by 10th Royal Inniskilling Fusiliers and withdrew to south of the Grid line E26 Central occupying the positions occupied on the night of the 21-11-1917.	
"	26		Refitting and resting	
"	27/28		Battalion was relieved by 1st Kings Liverpool Regiment and marched to Billets in BERTINCOURT and DOIGNIES.	
BERTINCOURT.	28		Battalion moved at 12 noon to BEAULENCOURT and was accommodated	

Army Form C. 2118.

WAR DIARY
INTELLIGENCE SUMMARY.
(Erase heading not required.)

Instructions regarding War Diaries and Intelligence Summaries are contained in F. S. Regs., Part II. and the Staff Manual respectively. Title pages will be prepared in manuscript.

Place	Date	Hour	Summary of Events and Information	Remarks and references to Appendices
BEAULENCOURT	29th		in huts. Battalion marched to BAPAUME and entrained at 2 P.M. for BEAUMETZ and marched to GOUY-en-ARTOIS arriving there at 6.50 P.M. and was accommodated in billets	
GOUY	30th		Notification received to Stand-by to move by Route march immediately at 12.15 P.M. Battalion left GOUY-en-ARTOIS at 3 P.M. and marched to ACHIET-la-PETITE arriving there at 10.30 P.M. and was accommodated in tents. Strength. Officers 51 Other Ranks 691	

In the Field
1st December, 1917.

[signature]
Lieut. Col.
Comdg. 11th (S.) Bn. Royal Inniskilling Fusiliers

11TH ROYAL INNISKILLING FUSILIERS.

WAR DIARY
FOR MONTH OF
DECEMBER, 1917.

Army Form C. 2118.

WAR DIARY 11th (S) Bn Rl Innis Fusl

December 1917

INTELLIGENCE SUMMARY.

(Erase heading not required.)

Instructions regarding War Diaries and Intelligence Summaries are contained in F.S. Regs., Part II. and the Staff Manual respectively. Title pages will be prepared in manuscript.

Place	Date	Hour	Summary of Events and Information	Remarks and references to Appendices
Achiet-le-Petit	1-12-17		Strength of Battalion 51 Officers 691 O.R.	
"	"		Battalion moved from Achiet-le-Petit at 4.5 P.m for Bancourt arriving there at 7 P.m. and was accommodated in tents	Appendix 1. Battalion Order
Bancourt	2-12-17		Battalion moved from Bancourt at 12 noon to Bertincourt arriving there at 2-45 P.M. and was accommodated in Biccles	No. 96. of 13-12-17 Appendix 2.
Bertincourt	3-12-17		Resting and cleaning	Battalion Order
"	4-12-17		Standing by to move at a moments notice. notification received to be ready to move if required. Battalion left Bertincourt at 9.0 a.m and arrived in HAVRINCOURT Wood Q14 at 11-30 a.m. where dinner was supplied, and moved off again at 3.0 P.m to E 31 and 32 (72.2)(HINDENBURG Support Line)	No 97. of 14-12-17 Battalion Order No. 99. of 25-12-17 Appendix 4
Trenches	5-12-17		Battalion moved into Brigade Reserve R.2.c.5.2. at 12 midnight	Divisional Comdr letter congratulating the Battn
"	6-12-17		Left trenches R.2.c.5.2. at 3.0 P.m and took over front-line trenches from 9th Rl Innis Fusiliers, who suffered heavily owing to successful German counter attack	Appendix 5.
"	7-12-17		Trenches heavily shelled by artillery fire. counter attack was organized and successfully carried out at 6.0 a.m	Brigadier General letter of sympathy to the Battalion

Army Form C. 2118.

WAR DIARY
or
INTELLIGENCE SUMMARY.

(Erase heading not required.)

1/6/1 Bn R. Lond Regt

December 1917

Instructions regarding War Diaries and Intelligence Summaries are contained in F.S. Regs., Part II, and the Staff Manual respectively. Title pages will be prepared in manuscript.

Place	Date	Hour	Summary of Events and Information	Remarks and references to Appendices
Trenches	7-12-17		The Battalion cleared 300 yards of trench on 200 yards front, thereby getting into touch with Battalions on their right and left, and straightening out an important sector of our line. The Battalion succeeded in retaining all ground gained though twice heavily counter attacked within 4 hours of gaining their objectives. Casualties - Killed 7 other ranks. Wounded 11 O.R.	
"	8-12-17		Trenches intermittently bombarded by artillery and trench mortars. Battalion was relieved by 10th R.S.R. 1 other Rank killed 7 other ranks wounded and went back to original front line.	
"	9-12-17		Working Parties.	
Metz	10-12-17		Battalion moved to METZ with the exception of Working Parties.	
"	11-12-17		Battalion resting. Working Parties joined Unit about 9.0pm	
"	12-12-17		Resting and cleaning	
"	13-12-17		Resting and cleaning. Notification received enemy intended to attack in strength at 6-30am. Battalion was ready to move if required at 6-0am. Battalion moved back to SOREL-LE-GRAND at 1-25pm	

Army Form C. 2118.

WAR DIARY
or
INTELLIGENCE SUMMARY.

(Erase heading not required.)

11th (S) Bn. Rl. Sussex Regt.

December 1917

Instructions regarding War Diaries and Intelligence Summaries are contained in F. S. Regs., Part II. and the Staff Manual respectively. Title pages will be prepared in manuscript.

Place	Date	Hour	Summary of Events and Information	Remarks and references to Appendices
Sorel le Grand	14-12-17		Resting and Cleaning	
"	15-12-17		Battalion moved to ROCQUIGNY arriving there at 2.45 pm	
ROCQUIGNY	16-12-17		Battalion moved to ETRICOURT and entrained there at 4 pm, detrained at	
"			MONDICOURT and marched to LUCHEUX	
LUCHEUX	17-12-17		Resting	
"	18-12-17		Companies at disposal of O.C. Coys. for cleaning, refitting etc	
"	19-12-17		Training and Recreational Training, 11-15 am to 12-30 pm Battalion Route March	
"			3 other ranks joined from Base	
"	20-12-17		Training and Recreational Training. 9 Officers joined from Reinforcement Camp	
"	21-12-17		Lecture by Commanding Officer, Gas Helmet Inspection.	
"			2nd Lieut. L. Schicabe proceeded for duty with Tanks Corps and struck off strength	
"	22-12-17		Training and Recreational Training, Medical Inspection. 1 O.Rs. joined from Reinforcement Camp	
"	23-12-17		Divine Service. Kit Inspection under supervision of Company Commanders	
"			15 other Ranks joined from Divl. Reinforcement Camp	
"	24-12-17		Training and Recreational Training. Battalion preparing for festivities on X-mas Day	

December 1917 WAR DIARY 11th (S) Bn Rl Innis Fus. Army Form C. 2118.

or

INTELLIGENCE SUMMARY.

(Erase heading not required.)

Place	Date	Hour	Summary of Events and Information	Remarks and references to Appendices
LUCHEUX	25-12-17		Christmas Day. Divine Service. Battalion assembled for dinner, followed by entertainment given Divisional Follies.	
"			Commanding Officer thanked all ranks for their loyal and willing support during recent operations, and wished every Officer, N.C.O. man a Happy Christmas & the best of Good Luck for 1918.	
"	26-12-17		Training and Recreational Training. Companies at disposal of O.C. Companies	
"	27-12-17		Training under Company arrangements. Notification received from the G.O.C. in Chief under the authority granted by His Majesty the King for the following decorations:—	
"			Bar to Military Medal	
			No. 14055 L/Sgt J R Edwards	
"			Military Medal	
			No. 14054 Sgt G Dick No. 17269 Pte A L Godfrey 14246 L/Cpl James W	
			" 11549 " R Armstrong 18952 " O. Tulip 18608 Cpl Fawkes F	
			" 14916 Pte R Neill 27573 " H Law +2001 Pte Tessaman J.	
				+3064 L/Cpl Gregory G.A	
			11545 " Keys T	

Army Form C. 2118.

December 1917 WAR DIARY 11th Bn. Royal Innis. Fus.
INTELLIGENCE SUMMARY

Instructions regarding War Diaries and Intelligence Summaries are contained in F. S. Regs., Part II. and the Staff Manual respectively. Title pages will be prepared in manuscript.

(Erase heading not required.)

Place	Date	Hour	Summary of Events and Information	Remarks and references to Appendices
AUCHEUX	28-12-17		Training. Battalion Route march. 1 Other Rank joined. 1 Officer Lieut. J. W. Chichton transferred to 9th Bn. Rl. Innis. Fus. 2 Other ranks joined from Reinforcement Camp. Battalion under orders to move.	
"	29/12/17		Battalion left AUCHEUX and entrained at MONDICOURT for MOREIUL arriving at new station 3-30 P.M. Lieut & Quartermaster D. J. Bell joined for duty	
MOREIUL	30-12-17		Divine Service	
"	31-12-17		Battalion Route march.	
			Strength Officers 59. Other Ranks 671	

In the Field
31-12-1917.

G. M. Hardy Major
Commanding 11th (S) Bn. Rl. Innis. Fus.

11TH ROYAL INNISKILLING FUSILIERS.

WAR DIARY

for

MONTH OF JANUARY, 1918.

WAR DIARY

of 11th (S) Bn Royal Inniskilling Fusiliers

INTELLIGENCE SUMMARY

(Erase heading not required.)

January 1918

Army Form C. 2118.

Place	Date	Hour	Summary of Events and Information	Remarks and references to Appendices
MOREUIL	1-1-18		Strength:- Officers 59 - Other Ranks 646. Training. Lewis Gun Class Instruction; Bombing and Rifle Grenading Instruction	
"	2-1-18		25 O.R's struck off strength. Training.- Route march.	H.S.
"	3-1-18		Training: Bayonet fighting and Physical Drill.	H.S.
"	4-1-18		Bathing. Training under Company Arrangements. 1 Officer + 1 O.R struck off Strength	H.S.
"	5-1-18		Training. Commanding Officer's Inspection of Battalion. Medical Inspection.	H.S.
"	"		41 O.R's struck off Strength.	
"	6-1-18		Divine Service. Kit inspection under Officer Commanding Companies. 2nd Lieut.	
"	"		J. Adair struck off Strength of Battalion having been invalided to Eng. (S). 6 O.R's	
"	"		arrived from Reinforcement Camp. 4 O.R's evacuated and struck off Strength.	H.S.
"	7-1-18		Battalion left MOREUIL at 10.30 a.m., and marched to VILLERS-aux-ERABLES arriving there same day.	H.S.
VILLERS-aux-ERABLES	8-1-18		Training. Lecture by Commanding Officer to all Officers and N.C.O's of Battalion.	H.S.
"	9-1-18		Battalion left VILLERS-aux-ERABLES. and marched to SOLENTE. 1 O.R, struck off strength.	H.S.

Army Form C. 2118.

WAR DIARY
or of the 11th (S). Bn. Royal Inniskilling Fusiliers
INTELLIGENCE SUMMARY.
(Erase heading not required.)

Instructions regarding War Diaries and Intelligence Summaries are contained in F. S. Regs., Part II. and the Staff Manual respectively. Title pages will be prepared in manuscript.

Place	Date	Hour	Summary of Events and Information	Remarks and references to Appendices
SELENTE	10-1-18		Training. Platoon inspection. Physical training and running exercises.	Aps 5
"	11-1-18		Battalion left billets at SELENTE and marched to new station, ST SIMON.	Aps 5
ST SIMON	12-1-18		Battalion left billets at ST SIMON, and marched to ESSIGNY STATION relieving the 28th Regt. (French) and was in Brigade Reserve. The Corps Commander awarded the military medal to the following 14031 Sgt. Cairns, T; 10192 Pte. Sweeney, J; 14478 Sgt. Nesbitt, A; 28902 Pte. Hughes, J.J;	Aps 5 Aps 5 Aps 5
	13-1-18.		Situation normal. Training	Aps 5
	14-1-18		Training. Routine work.	Aps 5
	15-1-18		Routine work.	Aps 5
	16-1-18		Routine work.	Aps 5
	17-1-18.		The Battalion relieved the 9th R. Inniskilling Fusiliers in the C/R of JEANNE d'ARC Sector.	Aps 5
	18-1-18.		Situation normal	Aps 5
	19-1-18		Situation normal.	Aps 5
	20-1-18		Situation normal. 2 O.R.s wounded.	Aps 5
Jeanne Ins	21-1-18		Battalion was relieved by 9th Royal Inniskilling Fusiliers in C/R of JEANNE D'ARC	Aps 5

Army Form C. 2118.

WAR DIARY
of 11th (S) Bn Royal Inniskilling Fusiliers
INTELLIGENCE SUMMARY.

(Erase heading not required.)

Instructions regarding War Diaries and Intelligence Summaries are contained in F. S. Regs., Part II. and the Staff Manual respectively. Title pages will be prepared in manuscript.

Place	Date	Hour	Summary of Events and Information	Remarks and references to Appendices
Trenches	21-1-18		Sub-sector and went back to Brigade Support relieving 10th Royal Inniskilling Fusiliers	A53.
	22-1-18		Routine work and working parties.	A53.
	23-1-18		Routine work and working parties.	A53.
	24-1-18		Routine work and working parties.	A53.
	25-1-18		Routine work and working parties.	A53.
	26-1-18		Routine work and working parties.	A53.
Trenches	27-1-18		Battalion relieved 9th Royal Inniskilling Fusiliers in JEANNE d'ARC Left Sub sector. Situation normal.	A53.
"	28-1-18		Situation normal.	A53.
"	29-1-18		Battalion was relieved by 2nd Bn The Royal Irish Rifles and marched back to ARTEMPS.	A53.
ARTEMPS	30-1-18		Cleaning and Bathing.	A53.
"	31-1-18		Bathing and working parties.	A53.
			Strength: 55 Officers 635 Other Ranks.	

31st January. 1918.

M Nutt
Lieut. Col.
Commanding 11th (S) Bn. Royal Inniskilling Fusiliers

RELIEF   ORDERS   17.1.18.
                - by -   F. 20.
       Major R.S. KNOX, D.S.O.
Commanding 10th (Service) Battalion Royal Inniskilling Fusiliers.
++

1.   The 14th Battalion Royal Irish Rifles will take
     over to-day the 17th January, 1918 as follows :-
     "C" Coy. 14th R. Ir. Rif. from "A" Coy. 10th R. Innis. Fus.,
     "D" "   "   " "   "   "   "B" "   "   "   "   "
     "A" "   "   " "   "   "   "C" "   "   "   "   "
     "B" "   "   " "   "   "   "D" "   "   "   "   "

2.   Our "A", "B", & "D" Companies will take over the
     positions vacated by the same Companies of the 14th Royal
     Irish Rifles respectively.
            Our "C" Company will take over from their "C"
     Company at the end of the BOYAU de la STATION, B.15.c.50.90.

3.   The 14th will come to Battalion Headquarters with-
     out guides. Guides from our Companies will report at dusk
     at Battalion Headquarters.
            "A" Company will send down to Battalion Headquarters
     1 guide per post for the two platoons in the Front Line and
     1 guide for Company Headquarters, and 1 guide for the 3rd
     platoon of the 14th for which accommodation must be found.
            "B" Company will send down 3 guides for 3 platoons
     to Battalion Headquarters and 1 for Company Headquarters to
     guide Company to Company Headquarters, and will have 1 guide
     per section ready at Company Headquarters to lead to the
     posts in the line.
            "C" Company will have 3 guides ready.
            "D"   "   "   "   "   "   "

4.   It will be noted that each Company of the 14th Royal
     Irish Rifles has 3 platoons, and Company Commanders are
     responsible for seeing that accommodation for each platoon
     is provided.

5.   "A" & "B" Companies will come out in their Gum
     Boots and change in Quarry at Battalion Headquarters, and
     dry Gum Boots will be taken up by the Front Line Companies
     of the 14th Royal Irish Rifles.

6.   Lewis Gun Magazines and Boxes will be handed over
     and receipts taken , also S.A.A. and Bombs.

7.   Transport will take back to new billets, Cooking
     utensils, Lewis Guns, Trench Kits and Orderly Room Boxes.

8.   Rations will be at New Area.

9.   Major E.H. BARTON will take down guides from "C"
     & "D" Companies to new area for all Companies, and if he can
     be spared an Officer should go from each Company.

10.   All Dugouts will be handed over scrupulously clean
     and sanitary, and receipts obtained.
            Dispositions, Maps, etc., will be very accurately
     and carefully handed over to relieving unit.

11.   Completion of relief will be sent in CODE to Battn.
     Headquarters by a word beginning with the Company letter as
     usual.

                        (Sgd)   J.A. Caskey,

                                2/Lieut. & A/Adjt.,

11th Royal Inniskilling Fusiliers.

WAR DIARY

for

MONTH OF FEBRUARY, 1918.

WAR DAIRY
of
11th (S) Battn. ROYAL INNISKILLING FUSILIERS

20th February, 1918.

VOLUME 29.

------------o------------

Army Form C. 2118.

WAR DIARY
or
INTELLIGENCE SUMMARY

11th (S). Bn. Rl. Inniskilling Fusiliers.

February. 1918.

(Erase heading not required.)

Instructions regarding War Diaries and Intelligence Summaries are contained in F. S. Regs., Part II. and the Staff Manual respectively. Title Pages will be prepared in manuscript.

Place	Date	Hour	Summary of Events and Information	Remarks and references to Appendices
ARTEMPS	1.2.18		Routine Work, notification received from the 36th Divisional Commander of the disbandment of the Battalion	A/B.
	2.2.18		Routine work and working parties	A/B.
	3.2.18		" "	A/B.
	4.2.18		" "	A/B.
	5.2.18		" "	A/B.
	6.2.18		" "	
	7.2.18		" "	
	8.2.18		20 Officers and 400 Other Ranks transferred to the 9th Bn. Rl. Inniskilling Fusiliers, the remainder formed into a Commande Company remained in ARTEMPS to do working parties. Battalion Headquarters + C.Q.M.S moved to VILLESELVE	A/B.
VILLESELVE	9.2.18		Routine work and working parties	A/B.
	10.2.18		" "	A/B.
	11.2.18		" "	A/B.
	12.2.18		" "	A/B.
	13.2.18		" "	A/B.
	14.2.18		" "	A/B.
	15.2.19		" "	A/B.

WAR DIARY
INTELLIGENCE SUMMARY

February 1918 11th (S) Bn R.I. Innis Killing Fusilrs

Army Form C. 2118.

Place	Date	Hour	Summary of Events and Information	Remarks and references to Appendices
VILLESELVE	16.2.18		Composite Company moved from ARTEMPS to GD SERAUCOURT. Routine Work and Working Parties	
	17.2.18		Routine Work & Working Parties	
	18.2.18		" " "	
	19.2.18		" " "	
CUGNY	20.2.18		Battalion Headquarters moved to CUGNY. Composite Coy Working Parties	
	21.2.18		Company at GD SERAUCOURT moved to CUGNY. All Officers with the exception of the 2nd in Command and 2nd in Command and all Other Ranks (30 Officers 219 Other Ranks) remaining with Battalion were amalgamated with the 14th Bn. R.I. Inniskg Rifles the whole forming the 23rd Entrenching Battalion under Lieut Col. O.R. VIVIAN. 1700 O.R. 9 W.Os & Staff Sgts Surplus to Base.	

W. Cust.
Lieut- Col
Comdg 11th (S) Bn R.I. Innis Killing Fusiliers

www.ingramcontent.com/pod-product-compliance
Lightning Source LLC
Chambersburg PA
CBHW080852230426
43662CB00013B/2082